MY SECRET
JOURNEY

MY SECRET JOURNEY

Renee Franklin

MY SECRET JOURNEY

Copyright © 2014 Renee Franklin.

iUniverse books may be ordered through booksellers or by contacting:

iUniverse
1663 Liberty Drive
Bloomington, IN 47403
www.iuniverse.com
1-800-Authors (1-800-288-4677)

Scripture quotations marked KJV are from the Holy Bible, King James Version (Authorized Version). First published in 1611. Quoted from the KJV Classic Reference Bible, Copyright © 1983 by The Zondervan Corporation.

ISBN: 978-1-4917-2653-2 (sc)
ISBN: 978-1-4917-2654-9 (e)

Print information available on the last page.

iUniverse rev. date: 05/14/2015

The following verses are my guide to teach people there is an answer for every problem through life's journey.

Help me o lord to follow your path the way I should live. I have chosen to obey. When I am going through storms I will obey the will of God faithfully and acknowledged him as the Lord. I know the Lord is smiling at me right now, because I will always honor my Lord with obedient he will always keep his promise for me because by his grace I will still stand. According to the teachings in the word of God being sure always because I will honor my Lord with an obedient heart he will always keep his promise because by his grace I will still stand. in everything we do we always seek the word of God he gone make me famous person one day with God on my site I will never lose I will be bless by the high favor God.

Obey and to follow his word. From King James translations' Psalm 46 God is our refuge and strength, a very present help in trouble. Verse 2 therefore will not we fear, though the earth be removed, and though the mountains be carried into the midst of the sea; verse 3 though the waters thereof roar and be troubled, though the mountains shake with the swelling thereof verse 4 there is a river, the streams whereof shall make glad the city of God, the holy place of the tabernacles of the most high. Verse 5 God is in the midst of her, she shall not be moved; God shall help her, and that right early, verse 6 the heathen raged, the kingdoms were moved; he uttered his voice the earth melted. Verse 7 The Lord of hosts is with us; the God of Jacob is our refuge, verse 8 come, beholds the works of the Lord, what desolation he hath made in the earth. Verse 9 He maketh wars to cease unto the end of the earth; he breaketh the bow, and cutteth the spear in sunder; he burneth the chariot in the fire. Verse 9 verses 10 be still and know I am God; I will be exalted among the heathen, I will be exalted in the earth, verse11 The Lord of hosts is with us, the God of Jacob is our refuge. KJT.

My name is Renee franklin I was born on July 2, 1968. I was a very small infant, at the time I was very ill, so bad the doctors thought that I wouldn't make it. My family prayed that day to Jesus for my recovery but God saved my life. It was a miracle! The doctors put ice on me and my fever went down and the rest his history. My sickness was a close call; the doctors provided me with special needs by God Grace. My mom and dad were afraid to take care of me because I was so tiny, so my grandma Millie took care of me until I got to be a big enough to go home. I was a healthy baby. My grandma fattened me up with her good home cooked meals. I love my grandma. She was very smart, always dedicated her life to the Lord. She always took me to church when I was tiny baby, she always made me laugh. She was funny to me, she was very smart, and she worked and took time to take to care of me too. I was 3 years old when my brother, Greg was born on June 1970. My grandma wanted me to go home to mom and dad so I can grow up with my brother. Grandma said "Darlene Renee is big UN snuff too take care now. It's about time you take her home. Darlene replied "ok Mom I'll Take Renee home today".

In 1972 February Paul was born. My mother and father were always working every day. Back then we had a babysitter every evening when we came home from school. Mom would fix us dinner and we watched cartoons and our baby sitter would put us to bed for a nap. My mom worked in the evenings and father worked also. We were bad when we were growing up but we did not know better; if we did not obey we got disciplined by our parents. It was back in early 70's winter time my mom and dad were at work and our baby sitter was in the front room playing notes on the organ. One time when we were about 3, 4, and 5 years old my brothers and I were throwing boots out the window. We saw a nice old Lady walk by; I think she was telling us we should not throw boots out the window. "Your mom and dad wouldn't like that". Renee "Hey would you throw the boots back to us?" She looked at us like 'what?' We were young did not know any better. When Mom found out we got a whipping. My mom got the belt out and we got disciplined that day. We never threw boots out the window again. Another time my brother and I got into the Christmas candy for the cookies in the middle of the night, about 12 or 3 am in the morning. We got caught. We got disciplined when we were bad, she lets us no its was tough love; From, Proverbs 19 verse 18 Please discipline your children why they at early stage if they don't learn now they will destroy themselves, if you don't help them enough.

My God had a destiny for my life, even though I went through all kinds of trouble. When growing up back in the days, being a special needs child wasn't easy; it was a very uncomfortable establishment being a slow learning child. My school put in special education class. This was not easy being accepted my friends. Toni turns on me; I mean she completely changed. Toni was very mean and horrible. She turned on me like I wasn't anybody. She was not the same person I use to know. Toni: "Renee ACAC" she telling me I was dummy. I was unable to speak on or defend myself in front of whole lots students. Embarrassed and ashamed I would drop my head and cry. I lost my friends, thinking I was underachiever un easy physical in mental pain I was discomfort, my hair fell out I' had to wear a wig to school, that's was very uncomfortably, for me, because the kids would pull it off my head and throw the wig in the middle of the street right in front of everybody out side, that's was so Embarrassed day of life, But God with me every step up the way, brother Greg was so of shame he run of head of me and head for the hills, I' re member on picture day my brother and I Were waking from school we almost at home and I fell in the summit in right in the middle in hole in the street, summit was all over me I said Greg help me once again my brother ran in left me in the hole, Greg was embassies of me again by the grace of God Jesus help me out the hole, I pull myself to safety, the people did not help me, they around looking But God, step in for my behalf, I' went home of look like of mess But God brought out of mess, By the grace of God he work threw my mom she wash me out with warm water and all the summit came off, But God save my life, KJB Isaiah 54 verse for thy maker is thine husband; the Lord of hosts is his name; and thy redeemer the holy one of Israel; The God of the whole earth shall he be called. KJT Isaiah 53 verse 10 for the mountains shall depart and the hills be removed; but my kindness shall not depart from thee, neither shall the covenant of my peace be removed, saith the Lord that hatch mercy on thee.

From the king James bible Isaiah 54 verse My Family really pray for me as well, my grandma Mildred always in courage me and help me not give up she always tell me about God, and not give up, when we were growing up we were all go to church all of the time, morning service evening services Sunday school, My mother would had prayer meeting on Friday night all night, in the summer are parents sent my brothers and I to Vacation Bible school back in the early in the late 70's there were lots church Tents outside in different community back in the days, that's really pay off, to me what's a better understanding about God's word at the time I really thank spending time more with God, But I' No he was real, I took time some time and read my bible and pray too, And my mother would help my brothers and I to pray to the Lord in prayer in the book of Matthew.

September or October 1983. God was my solution to my problem, I gave my life to Jesus when I' was 12 or 13 years old, at the time, are pastor call us up for alter call at church so we can give are lives to Christ, so my parents and my brothers and me went up for to reseed salvation to be save, from sin, being Christ like was not easy, But my hope was with God to help me, God do everything but failed, KJB Ecclesiastes 12 verse 1 Remember now thy creator in the days of thy youth, verse 2 while the sun, or the light, or the moon, or the stars, be not darkened, nor the clouds return after the rain; verse 3 in the day when the keepers of the house shall tremble, and the strong men shall bow themselves, and the grinders cease because they are few, and those that look out of the windows be darkened, verse 4 and the doors shall be shut in the streets, when the sound of the grinding is low, and he shall rise up at the voice of the bird, and all the daughters of musick shall be brought low; verse 5 also when they shall be afraid of that which is high, and fears shall be in the way, and the algrasshopper shall be burden, and desire shall fail; because man goeth to his long home, and the mourners go about the streets; from King James Bible, Deuteronomy 8 KJB verse 6 Therefore thou shalt keep the commandments of the Lord thy God, to walk in his ways, and to fear him. verse 7-8 for the lord thy God bringeth thee into a good land, a land of brooks of water, of fountains and depths that spring out of valleys and hills, a land of wheat, and barley, and vines, and fig trees, and pomegranates. a land of oil olive, and honey; knowing God was the best thing that's ever happen to me my Jesus is concern about my family and I' we experienced storms to get close to God, we all good days, and bad days don't we all, but God always make of way out, I remember my mom and my grand mom took me to the mall fall 1979 is my first time getting my ears pierced this man had like of gun like, he tells me you won't feel a thing in my ears my mom and my grand mom encouraged me you gone be fine I was 9 years old at the time there was an audience, everybody at the mall look I was sinner of tension like feeling like a movie star I' mean the whole mall had they eyes on me, at the time getting my ears pierced they make me feel good about myself like God was display me that day, God let me know, From the good bible, from KJB Proverbs 31 verse favour is deceitful and beauty is vain but a woman that feareth the Lord, she shall be praised. Give her of the fruit of her hands; and let her own works praise her in the gates. KJB. From the Isaiah 60 verse 1the spirit of the Lord God is upon me; because the Lord hath anointed me to preach good tidings unto the meek; he hath sent me to bind up the broken hearted, to proclaim liberty to the captives, and them that are bound, and the gentiles shall come to thy light, and kings to the brightness of thy rising. Verse3 we had lots of birthday party back then, my father side of the family, my grandma and granddaddy and my family every holiday season, we be there, Christmas time between 1970's or 80's, my father and my uncle's try to barbecued a turkey on the grill outside in the winter time they never could cook, my whole family laugh because they know could it be done, My aunts my mom and whole family would had a good relationship my cozens and I would play cards, and have a good time My father was tough he did not take no mess, my mom was too, back in the days my father an my uncles love to drink. they would take the floor, one time my uncle James brought a big bottle of wine for to celebrate my father birthday, my father did not let no one touch the bottle of wine until it was all gone, my uncle James try to take the bottle away from my daddy my daddy grab the bottle from his brother hands, my father gets mad and said if you take his wine or even Dow the wine was my uncle no one mess with the wine until my father drink it all, he was gone to beat up my uncle, James did not won't to fight so he sit down somewhere and he did say a another word about the wine, when my father was in the bar a man come at him with a gun, my father was in his 20's at the time my father grab the man's gun and beet the man so bad, he never came at my father again Matter of fact the man told my daddy he was sorry and brought my daddy a drink. and he made acquaintance with him My God had my dad cover, But God, May be it might been back in 1960's I' re member the time my cozen would tell story about my father when we were going up, one time Billy my cozen told us about the story about they hell up a white people bar back in the days before silver rights. Granddaddy thought they was in trouble but come to find out my dad and the others was starting trouble so my granddaddy got is shot gun to drive to the white people bar as fast as he can and daddy and are other cozen hell up a white bar say this is stick up they did hurt no body they just stolen some whiskey and wine that's all they wanted my granddad was very upset and he might of told them you know better than to do something dump like that you all could got kill in site at the time, and one time cozen Billy told us my daddy had come of tat ion with a man when he was in the army the man start a fight with my daddy the man say to him he gone to hurt my dad, and for you know it my father grab the man and pull in lock he learn in the army and the man try brake free but my dad did let go, noting could my dad said to him so you gone to hurt me, you know not to mess with me I'm put my foot in your, then cozen Lou and uncle Leroy hay, Greg lets the man go, it took uncle Leroy an cozen Lou to pull my father off that man it took a good while then finely daddy set him free, that man no not mess with my dad again he count holey catch his breath, his friends say let's get out of here, Greg, My mom did take no mess either when we was going up back 1985 we know some white people next doors to us they was some trouble makers they use to like us but they turn on us, they kids was bad, we always get into with the Johnson's, they pick with us in hole neighborhood, far back that I can remember we was on the playground my brother was about 12 miss Johnson son Bobbie was throwing rocks at my brother Paul and Bobbie was 17 years old almost a man very tall 'I was very small about 5'4 I' as I was walking to the playground I saw what he was doing to my brother saying don't do that and Bobbie did not pay me no mind then I beat the mess out Bobbie, and one time his sister try to stage a scene in front of her friends when we were coming from school. Her name was sally she came at me for no reason at all I told her 'I did want to hit her she try to hit me and I' wear her out I beat her up bad, her mom came running out the house, and miss Johnson try to come at me, then my mom friend pull up her other neighbor Linda say if you hit that little girl I' gone hit you, then miss Johnson turn around and sally went back in the house, My mom herd what happen that day when she coming home from t work, and dad also were not to please, One night we all sitting outside are neighbor and my family on a Saturday about 8 or 9pm miss jobson came at my mother again for no reason how to describe what happen miss Johnson got in my mom face she try to hit my mom and she miss and mom beat her up and threw her on the ground and miss Johnson was so scared to get up she lay there until my mom walk away, then everything was over mister Johnson yell at his wife to get up off the ground, everybody outside was cheering to mom for put miss Johnson in her place, My father was scared for my mom he thought she might go to jail, the Johnson call about 5 police cars out there, the police was so tire of them they call them every Saturday for same oh thing about something, What is it this time one of them say, Until this day Paul my brother still love to talk about, Court day came up my mom and dad went to court we did lots praying for that day came are pastor are friends and are family we had a lots of support that day, But God had a plan, for my parents, that day KJB Isaiah 29 verse 15 woe unto them that seek deep to hide their counsel from the Lord and their works are in the dark, and they say, who seeth? Us and who knoweth us? And who verse 16 surely your turning of things upside down shall be esteemed as the potter's clay; for shall the work say of him that made it, he made me not? Or shall the thing framed say of him that frame it, he had no understanding? Verse 22 Therefore thus saith the Lord, who redeemed Abraham, concerning the house of Jacob, Jacob shall not now be ashamed, neither shall his face now wax pale. And then the people coming in the court room the judge was walking in everybody rise; the judge saying to them you may be seated. then the while came miss Johnson took the stand she was lying after lying, after she spoke and her lawyer he says no furrier question you sit down now. the Johnson thought they was wining, and all miss Johnson friends was sitting down, they had look on the face, like what you talking about, one by one they took the stand. something All son happen, miss Johnson friends were on my mom site the table turn on her, all the witness toe everything the Johnson had did I' mean every detail then something happen the Lady live two doors from us was very ill the people had to pull in the wheel chair in the court room, its miss Johnson friend, miss Lawson, miss Lawson provide the judge information no body know about, the Audience was in silence she actually spoke what was said be hide close doors, after she spoke the judge threw the case out the court and disc miss all the charkhas, were drop, win you got God you can't lose, KJB Genesis 18 verse 4 is anything too hard for the Lord? Jeremiah 33 verses 14 Behold, the days come, saith the Lord that I will perform that good thing which I have promised unto the house of Israel and to the house of Judah.

Back in the days in the early 80's 1983 84 I did not date that mush. When I was going up this nice guy I use had crush on, his name was James I met him in church he was very neat hair combed and very quiet, he was much older than me he was 17 and I was 13 he use watch me every Sunday at church, matter of fact James fell in love with me, when we use site together in church my dad would come over and get me and have me site next to my mom and my brothers my father was very carefully he would keep his eye on James like hawk, my mom and dad then care to mush for him, at the time my father was a privet detective at the time. He found him out James was not a very good person. He love me so much he ask my mom and dad for my hand in marriage, in his country it was license to get married at 18 and 13years old of age, my father toe James I was too young to get married, you don't have are approval, stay away from my doubter, James walk out and drove away back to his hometown he join the army. And I never heard or seen him again. My brother Paul was bad when he was little he got kick in all of the time in school in Ohio. One time he got expel from school from fighting and the teacher send the letter to my parents to let them know he got expelled from school but my parents never know about it my brother would hang out at the playground everyday like he was going to school. And stay close to nearby to catch the mailman to get the note that the teacher send by the mail and Paul got the letter too. Until this day my dad never found out, backs in the late 1970's now back 1986 in high school my brother is in class and the teacher said I would like some donuts right of the middle of class. His teacher mister smith ask Paul run down to the donuts shop and by a big box of donuts and brother said ok I thank the teacher gave Paul some money to go pay for the donuts my brother drove to donuts shops, when Paul came back the dean called Paul to his office he said why did you leave the school, my brother said mister smith had taste for some donuts and he send to the donuts shop to get a box of donuts. And the dean had smell the donuts at the door those donuts look and smell good The dean said if you give me a donuts I won't expel you ok my brother mite of said, if my parents would knew that they would knock cross of street. Psalm 4 verse 12 for thou, Lord wilt bless the righteous; with favour wilt thou compass him as with a shield. Matthew 9 verse 28 believes ye that I am able to do this. God always come through for my family and I my parent were always praying for us my older brother Greg Had a close call to when he was growing up why he was playing football outside with his friends in our old place where we use to live my brother ran in to a pole he mess up his chin but God hill him he doing just find by the grace of God, he had a roll of recovery, as for me I had a close call I came close Call. I tried to kill myself with pills and I live d and got hit by car when I was 7 or 8 years of age. I almost got kidnapped when I was about 22 at years at age when I was working at the bakery. In 1992, I was almost killed; at the one wrong place at the wrong time and I could got shot that night when someone shot our family house that night if I would got out the bed I would not be here at this moment. We were so scared; we all were in shock. The men who shot our house were in the gang, the police came out and spoke to us and ask us were there gang members was the blame for shooting these house and those too home to next to you as well. We said no Greg knew who they are. See he bet up one the gang member were picking with him a couple of days ago. My big brother knew what went down Greg did mention a word to the police about what really happen he was afraid that's we be worried. For ye shall not go out with haste, nor go by flight; for the Lord will go before you; and the God of Israel will be your rereward, KJB Isaiah 52 verse 12 Back in 1992 I got a job working in the grocery store as a bakery girl by decoration the donuts I was so happy I always won't to work in the bakery because my grandmamma use to work in the bakery so I want do this I was train and I have the hang of it I was so proud of myself my Parents were so happy for me Because I thought I would never would work I work in the past before but at the time this was my favored job. Are parents taunt us the value of life to be impendent to help us to find our own way of live my mom and my grand mom and daddy would say to me and my brothers you have to learn how do things on your own we will not always be around to help you what's you gone to do when we die When my father and my mother forsake me, then the Lord will take me up. KJB. Psalm 27 verse 10 We all had our own Jobs we all had nice cars and good paying jobs, we all of us we all did good we never got in trouble and we never went to jail or at the court house we were all living large, my mom taught us how to pay bills and to live on our own. And she always tells us to stay with God and is everyday life. We were not perfect but we serve a perfect God and that's what matter the most. My Parents refuse to have slow child. She taught us well. Matthew 5 verse 10 Blessed are they which are persecuted for righteousness' sake; for theirs is the kingdom of heaven, KJB I had hard time when I was going up people were so dirty and mean to me all of the time in my storms, But God always made way out of my hard times now back when I was working at the bakery back in 1992 my manager gave a hard time and treated me cruelly, But God show up for me every time, The Lord is my light and my salvation; whom shall I fear? The Lord is the strength of my life; of whom shall I be afraid? When the wicked, even mine enemies and my foes, came upon me to eat up my flesh, they stumbled and fell. Though an host should encamp against me, my heart shall not fear; though war should rise against me, in this will I be confident. KJB Psalm 27 verse 1-2-3 one Morning about 2.am. I clock in for the day as I walking in the kitchen not person was in site at all so I try to call the manger there was no answer. When I hung up saying what to do so I start walking around the store looking for someone for someone to help me not one person was there not even a customer in site. When I was going through a storm God is on my side and he on watch he will entangle me out of trouble I will not fear. He will give me the strength to wait. So I wait then time past about 3or 4 am Lee walk in soon he clock in I said we need donuts right away, he said I will cook the right away, time past again the mangers walk in and she was saying was Lee on the work sheet and mite of said that's what it said she had funny look on her face her plan backfire on her. When you have Jesus you can't lose. After while they fire me saying I did know what I doing on the Job saying I did not know the different between Custer and cream frosting or they would say I was doing a good job they will give full time, they was telling me all kind of lies, Psalms112 KJB verse 6-7 Surely he shall not be moved for ever; the righteous shall be in everlasting remembrance. He shall not be afraid of evil tidings; his heart is fixed, trusting in the Lord. He hath dispersed, he hath given to the poor; his righteousness endureth for ever; his horn shall be exalted with honour. Verse 10 The wicked shall see it, and be grieved; he shall gnash with his teeth, and melt away; the desire of the wicked shall perish, there know hope for them weeks later the company shut down all the people did me wrong did have a job Psalm 37 KJB verse 7 Rest in the Lord and wait patiently for him; fret not thyself because of him who prospereth in his way because of the man who bringeth wicked devices to pass. KJB Psalm 40 verse 1 I wait patiently for the Lord and He inclined into me and heard my cry.

Proverbs 16 KJB. In one of the chapter we can make are plans but God will give us the right answer. Verse 2 The preparations of the heart in man, and the answer of the tongue, is from the Lord. Verse 4 the Lord hath made all things for himself; yea, even the wicked for the day of evil.

Today is Wednesday 23rd 211 on thanksgiving eve. About 958 am the morning I got up in took a shower and felt my cat and press God for a another day God is good all the time he Worley to be press I Give Jesus all the glory and honor and press he is good for every day his love mercy doing for ever I give thanks because he good. I know God gone display one day God gone do a brand new thing for me and my family someday He gone make the smallest family A mighty nation someday, KJB ISAIAH 60 verse 22 A little one shall become a thousand, and a small one a strong nation; I the Lord will hasten it in his time. KJB PSALM 37 verses 18 The Lord knoweth the days of the upright; and their inheritance shall be for ever. Verse 19 They should not be ashamed in the evil time and in the days of famine they shall be satisfied. I pray to God to help me today that's all I can do no matter how I go through storms I still press god what I going threw I don't blame him for nothing but I press God anyhow I know what he done for me in my past God brought this far he not gone leve me now, is very importance to trust in Jesus in my everyday life when are on are journey KJB Psalm 37 verse 3 Trust in the Lord and do good; so shalt thou dwell in the land, and verily thou shalt be fed. Verse 4 delight thyself also in the Lord; and he shall give thee the desires of thine heart. Verse 5 commit thy way unto the Lord trust also in him, and he shall bring it to pass. Verse 6 and he shall bring forth thy righteousness as the light, and thy judgment as the noonday. Oh Lord Help I meditate on the word of God. I am and not perfect but God is perfect he never lie or change his mine but God keeps his promise JOHN

14 KJB Jesus saith unto him, I am the way, the truth, and the life. No man come unto the father but by me. NUMBERS 23 VERSE 19 God is not like man who lie he not people who changes his mine, 20 verse whatever he says he speaks, come to pass it has been instructed already to bless he cannot take it back as he promises. His will shall be fulfill. 20 KJB JOHN 14 verse 1 let your heart be troubled; Verse 2 Ye believe in God, believe also in me. In my father's house are many mansions; if it were not so, I would have told you. I go to prepare a place for you. And if I go and prepare a place for you, I will come again, and receive you unto myself; that where I am there ye may be also. And whither I go ye know, ye know, and the way ye know. Verse 5 Thomas saith unto him, Lord, we know not whither thou goest; and how can we know the way? Verse 6 Jesus saith unto him, I am the way, the truth, and the life; no man cometh unto the father, but by me. KJB ISAIAH 41 VERSE 8 But thou, Israel, art my servent Jacob whom I have chosen, the seed of Abraham my friend. VERSE 9 thou whom I have taken from the ends of the earth, and called thee from the chief men thereof and said unto thee, thou art my servant; I have chosen thee, and not cast thee away. KJB ISAIAH 43 VERSES 13 Yea before the day was I am he; and there is none that can deliver out of my hand; I am He and there is none that can deliver out of my hand I will work and who shall let it? KJB ISAIAH 59 VERS 16 and he saw that there was no man, and wondered that there was no intercessor; therefore his arm brought salvation unto him; and his righteousness, it sustained him. KJB Isaiah 43 VERSE 11 I, even I, am the Lord; and beside me there is no savior. There no one greater than my God he is real and for live forever on time and always on time his arrival will never be forgot ting be the glory of history in perfect season when God will always show up for my family and I my Jesus is very important to me in my life every day journey this the day that's the Lord has made lets us rejoice and be glade it is. Now is about 801 pm I am set for now I made A Good Thanksgiving meal Today Chicken stuffing yams macaroni and cheese claw slaw and cranberry sauce, did not feel very well this holiday I miss mom and grand mom and my dead love ones are not here, but God is here with me threw though time I still trust and press God for a another night He did have to let me live but he have to live but God let me see a another day, one more time, I ACKNOWLEDGE your name Jesus Psalm

91 verse 4 KJB HE SHALL COVER THEE WITH HIS FEATHERS, AND UNDER HIS WINGS SHALT THOU TRUST; HIS TRUTH SHALL BE THY SHIELD AND BUCKLER. 15 He shall call upon me, and I will answer him; I will be with him in trouble; I will deliver him, and honour him. my goal in my life is seek God in my life and my family continue to seek the Lord as well. And pray for others to seek God and many more people I pray for every day well I try to pray, sometimes I don't pray like I sure but I refuse to give up on God He change a sinner like me and he can change other to. Whoever put their trust in God will never be put to shame, as the deer pets for stream of water so I long for you Oh Lord I try my best to seek my Lord by fasting, praying, obeying in what I try to do when I pray I say let God's will be done. My goal in life to encourage others there is hope in God if I can make it so can others as well. With God on my side I can make it, I can do all things through Christ who strengthens in me Philippians 4:13. I so many goals in my life I won't to help other as well first I put Jesus first in my life and my curial and I won't to help other what I been threw to courage them there hope in Christ KJB JEREMIAH 15 VERSE 19 THEREFORE THUS SAITH THE LORD, IF THOU RETURN, THEN WILL I BRING THEE AGAIN, AND IF THOU SHALT STAND BEFORE ME; AND IF THOU TAKE FORTH THE PRECIOUS FROM THE VILE, THOU SHALT BE AS MY MOUTH; LET THEM RETURN UNTO THEE ; BUT RETURN NOT THOU UNTO THEM. JEREMIAH 6 VERSE 16 KJB Thus saith the Lord, stand ye in the ways, and see, and ask for the old paths, where is the good way, and walk therein, and ye shall find rest for your souls, but they said, we will not walk therein. KJB JEREMIAH 15 VERSE 11 The Lord said, verily it shall be well with thy remnant; KJB JEREMIAH 29 VERSE 11 for I know the thoughts that I think toward you, saith the Lord thoughts of peace, and not of evil, to give you an expected end. 12 Then shall ye call upon me, and ye shall go and pray unto me, and I will hearken unto you. VERSE 14 and I will be found of you, saith the Lord and I will turn away your captivity, and I will gather you from all the nations, and from all the places whither I HAVE DRIVEN YOU, SAITH THE LORD; I BEIVE IN GOD WORD IS POWER THAN A TO EGE Sword

December 12, 2011, Monday. I had a good day and a bad day, but God keep his promise and he help me every step of the way I went through a storm but God work it out for me always. For the Lord taketh pleasure in his people ; he will beautify the meek with salvation. KJB PSALM 149 VERSE;4 KJB PSALM 91 VERSE 16 With long life will I satisfy him, and shew him my salvation. So God always have a word for me he always make my day. THE LORD WILL BLESS HIS PEOPLE WITH PEACE. KJB PSALM 29 VERSES 11 THE LORD WILL GIVE STRENGTH UNTO HIS PEOPLE; THE LORD WILL BLESS HIS PEOPLE WITH PEACE. THOU WILT KEEP HIM IN PERFECT PEACE, WHOSE MIND IS STAYED ON THEE; BECAUSE HE TRUSTETH IN THEE. TRUST YE IN THE LORD JEHOVAH IS EVERLASTING STRENGTH. KJB ISAIAH 26 VERSES 3-4 Romans 6 verse 22 KJB But now being made free from sin, and become servants to God, ye have your fruit unto holiness, and the end everlasting life. My goals to be all that God won't me to be to do his will whatever God will be for me lets his will be done. My list for my strengths is I won't help other and courage them there is hope in Christ 2 being a leader let people know not to give up, and put God first you never being in need my three weaknesses' some time I feel alone depress I eat things I should not eat, Three goals that come with strengths or weaknesses to think and fill good about my fur sure and look for a brighter tomorrow and eat right and excise and reaching my goals is to lose weight and maybe someday if is God will I will become a teacher for the Lord and witness to other people to let them there is hope in Christ Jesus, or be in outreach program and turn over a new leave in life. And become an actress and sell and decorate coffee mugs and have on cooking show or have my own gift shop. And I would frame my goals and continuous and enhance my life daily by trusting God for help and look at myself all my days I CAN DO ALL THIHGS THROUGH CHRIST WHICH STRENGTHENETH ME. KJB PHILIPPIANS 4-13 That God word for the day, MY journeys for the day is walking in the word of God scriptures for this day KJB Matthew 9 verse 28 Believe ye that I am able to do this? KJB Psalm27 verses 11 teach me thy way, o Lord, and lead me in a plain path, because of mine enemies. Verse 12 Deliver me not over unto the will of mine enemies; for false witnesses are risen up against me, and such as fainted, unless I had believed to see the goodness of the Lord in the land of the living. KJB Jeremiah2 verse 3 Israel was holiness unto the Lord, and the first fruits of his increase; all that devour him shall offend; evil shall come upon them, saith the Lord,

Matthew 18 KJB verse 19 again I say unto you, that if two of you shall agree on earth as touching anything that they shall ask, it shall be done for them of my Father which is in heaven. Verse 20 for where two or three are gathered together in my name, there am I in the midst of them. Verse 18 verily I say unto you, whatsoever ye shall bind on earth shall bound in heaven; and whatsoever ye shall loose on earth shall be loosed in heaven. God always come through for my family and I would always pray for us all of the time because God always answer prayer. There's hope in Jesus KJB Mark 11 verse 23 for verily I say unto you, that whosoever shall say unto this mountain, be thou removed, and be thou cast into the sea; and shall not doubt in his heart, but shall believe that those things which he saith shall come to pass; he shall whatsoever he saith. Verse 24 Therefore I say unto you, what things soever that ye desire, when ye pray, believe that ye receive them, and shall have them. Verse 25 and when ye stand praying, forgive, if ye have ought against any; that your Father also which is in heaven may forgive you your trespasses. God is able his will be done in O lord, so many are against me. So many seek to harm me I Have so many enemies, so many say that God will never help me. But lord, you are my shied. My glory and my only hope. KJB You alone can lift my head now bowed in shame Psalms 3 verse 1-2-3-Lord how are they increased that trouble me! Many are they that rise up against me. Many there be which say of my soul, there is no help for him in God.

But thou, o lord, art a shied for me; my glory, and the lifter up of mine head. I cried unto the Lord with my voice, and he heard me out of his holy hill, KJB Psalms 3 verse 4 be And a year later the, KJB PSALM 46 verse 10 be still and know, I am God, verse 1God is our refuge and strength, a very present help in trouble. Verse 2 a Therefore will not we fear so thank positive according to God word. Trust God always in every prayer because God will answer you without delay Jesus keeps his promise nothing compare to promise, take look back in your past and say my future looks great Jesus not gone to leave us this far and leave us by are self now, But seek ye first the kingdom of God. And his righteousness; and all these things shall be added unto you. KJB Matthew 6 verse 33 So commit to God, would you pray in seek him with all your heart today, growing close to God that's God plan for are everyday life journey. So make speaking terms with God and you never go wrong. Obey that's the main key that's what he won't us to do. So cheer up put a smile on your face and look up and say God will make my name great, and praise God. But it is good for me to draw near to God; I have put my trust in the Lord God, that I may declare all thy works. KJB Psalm 73 verse 28 Take from me God help me. He will help you too. Jesus is reliable at all times KJB Jeremiah 15 verse 11 The Lord said, verity it shall be well with thy remnant; verily, Jeremiah17 VERSE 7 Blessed is the man that trusteth in the Lord, and whose hope the Lord is. KJB Numbers 23 verse 19.

God is not a man, that he should lie; neither the son of man, that he should repent; hath he said, and shall he not do it? Or hath he spoken, and shall he not make it good? Verse 21 He hath not beheld iniquity in Jacob, neither hath he seen perverseness in Israel; the Lord his God is with him, and the shout of a king is among them, KJB Hebrews 13 verse 5 for he hath said, I will never leave thee, nor forsake thee. Believe in the possible. KJB Jeremiah 31 verse 17 And there is hope in thine end, said the Lord, KJB Proverbs 30 verse 5 every word of God is pure; he is a shied unto them that put their trust in him. No matter who you are race or if you have an education or not, God will have a great future for your life. Circumstances will change in time only God will have a connection for your future; Opportunity is headed your way. You have a good chance with Jesus you're marked with a blessing. During your time of trouble, KJB Mark 11 verse 24 Therefore I say unto you, what things soever ye desire, when ye pray, believe that ye receive them, and ye shall have them. verse 25 and when ye stand praying, forgive, that your Father also which is in heaven may forgive you your trespasses. KJB Psalm 69 verse Save me, o God; for the waters are come in unto my soul. I sink in deep mire, where there is no standing; I am come in into deep waters, where the floods overflow me. I am weary of my crying; my throat is dried; mine Regardless how bad your luck looks trust God He will never fail you while I wait for my God. He will Come through for you if you only believe, according to God's plan. KJB Philippians 4 verse 19 but my God shall supply all your need according to his riches in glory by Christ Jesus. KJB Philippians 1 verse 4 Always in every of mine for you all making request with joy, verse 6 being confident of this very thing, that he which hath began a good work in you will perform it until the day of Jesus Christ; Today is a fresh start. Praying to Jesus is the guide us every day today life forever, KJB Proverbs 8 verse 17 I love them that love me; and those that seek me early shall find me, Riches and honour are with me; yea durable riches and righteousness. Verse 34 blessed is the man that heareth me, wating at the posts of my doors, verse 35 for whoso findeth me findeth life, and shall obtain favdeth of the Lord. verse 36But he that sinneth against me wrongeth his own soul; all they that hate me love death. KJB John 12 verse I am come a light into the world, that whosoever believeth on me should not abide in darkness. 46 verse 47 and if any man hear my words, and believe not, I judge him not; for I came not to judge the world, but to save the world I came not to judge the world. Verse 48 He that rejecteth me, and receiveth not my words, hath one that judgeth him; the word that I have spoken, the same shall judge him in the last day. And I know that his commandment is life everlasting; whatsoever I speak therefore even as the father said unto me, so I speak. KJB Genesis 18 verse 14 is anything too hard for the Lord. KJB Matthew 28 verse 2O I am with you always, even unto the end of the world; my For David speaketh concerning him, I foresaw the Lord always before my face, for he is on my right hand, that I should not be moved; KJB Acts 2-25-26 I had an encounter on my other job in my other season where I use to work back in the days one other time. But God is in control let me tell you what had happen. I had an encounter on my job and the past with my bosses they were so mean it would even funny they did me bad so much the yell at me and push me and try to set me up and lie on me and did said all kind of bad stuff about me was not true, they would make me work by myself outside in the rain and the heat in 90s degree weather in outside by myself sometimes the customers would come to help me push the carts and clean the snow most of the time outside the grocery store even sometimes I was discouraged God had my back every time my hope is in God, the lord is near to those who are discouraged, he saves those who have lost all hope. KJB Psalm 34 verse 17-18 The righteous cry, and the Lord heareth, and delivereth them out of all their troubles. The Lord is night unto them that are of a broken heart; and saveth such as be of a contrite spirit. Proverbs 3 KJB verse 26 For the Lord shall be thy foot from being taken. they try to do that to me trying to set me up but God show up every time, one day I was outside shoveling the snow one of the bosses wanted me to sweep that snow mountain out in the back of the store at the time I thought I could do the Job. But Jesus knew the manger no I could not do the job, So the lord sent supervision out nowhere and God show up with a snow trunk and wipe all the snow mountain on the top up the hill, and it was done by God. KJB Isaiah 41 verse 8 But thou, Israel art my servant, Jacob whom I have chosen, the seed of Abraham my fried. verse 9 Thou of I have taken from the ends of the chief men thereof, and said unto thee, thou art my servant; I have chosen thee, and not cast thee away. Verse 10 Fear thou not; for I am with thee; be not dismayed; for I am thy God; I will strengthen thee; yea, I will help yea, I will uphold thee with the right hand of my righteousness. KJB Jeremiah 17 verse 7 Blessed is the man that trusteth in the Lord, whose hope the Lord is. I went through hard times and storms and all kind of troubles and suffering I Still praise God when I going through, I don't blame him for nothing but I praise him for everything those people may get by with me but they will not get by God. Deuteronomy KJB 32 verse 35 To me belongeth vengeance, and recompence; their foot shall slide in due time; for the day of their calamity is hand, and the things that shall For David speaketh concerning him I foresaw the Lord always before my face, for he is on my right hand, that I should not be moved; KJB Acts 2-25 Those people did me wrong at my old job what they did to me came back on them. They all got they pay back one man got fire he was accords out the building by security on the job and the other manger married an alcoholic a another was fire as well and other one had a nerves breakdown. What they did to me Woe unto them that deep to hide their work are in the dark, and they say, who seeth us! And who knowth us? boomerang on them For the terrible one is brought to nought, and the secorner is consumed, and all that watch for iniquity are cut off. Isaiah 29 verse 20 Verse 21 That make a man an offender for a word, and lay a snare for him that approveth in the gate. And turn aside the just for a thing of nought. KJB Isaiah 29 verse-15-20-21-22 Therefore thus saith the Lord who redeemed Abraham, concerning the house of Jacob, Jacob shall not now be ashamed, neither shall his face now wax pale. Jeremiah 6 verse 16 Thus saith the Lord, stand ye in the ways, and see, and ask for the old paths, where is the good way. KJB Jeremiah 1 verse 8 Be not afraid of their face; for I am with thee to deliver thee, saith the Lord. God keeps his request he always answer are prayer in time of need Great is my glorying of you; I am filled with comfort, I am exceeding joyful in all our tribulation. 2 KJB Corinthians 7 verse 4 my goals is to help others let them know there hope in God favors never will end, fear not; for I am with thee; I will bring thy seed from the east, and gather thee from the west, Isaiah 43 verse KJB 5 But God show up for me again. When God move he does it quickly.

Matthew 28 verse 20 I am with you always, even unto the end of the world. KJB

My God keeps his promise he has is watchful eyes is on me every day, KJB 2Samuel 7 verse 27 For thou, O Lord of hosts, God of Israel, hast revealed to thy servant, saying, I will build thee an house; therefore hath thy servant found in his heart to pray this prayer unto thee. Verse 28 And now, O Lord God, thou art that God and thy words be true, and thou hast promised this goodness unto thy servant; God had my back every time. The Lord is night unto them that are of a broken heart; and saveth such as be of a contrite spirt. Verse 19 many are the afflictions of the righteous; but the Lord delivereth him out them all, KJB Psalm 34 verse 18 be not afraid of sudden fear, neither of the desolation of the wicked, when it cometh. KJB Proverbs 3 verse 25 verse 26 for the Lord shall be thy confidence, and shall keep thy foot from being taken. KJB Isaiah 41 verse 8 but thou, Israel, art my servant Jacob whom I have chosen the seed of Abraham my friend. Verse 9 Thou whom I have taken from the ends of the earth. And called thee from the chief men thereof, and said unto thee, thou art my servant; I have chosen thee and not cast thee away. Verse 10 Fear thou not; for I am thy God; I will strengthen thee; yea, I will help thee; yea. I will uphold thee with the right hand of my righteousness. KJB Jeremiah 17 verse 7 Blessed is the man that trusteth in the Lord, and whose hope the Lord is verse 8 for he shall be as a tree planted by the waters, and that spreadeth out her roots by the river, and shall be when heat cometh, but her leaf shall be green; and shall not be careful in the year of drought, neither shall cease from yielding fruit. I went through hard time and storms and all kind of troubles and suffering I still praise God when I going through, I don't blame him for nothing but I praising him for everything, I went through a storm Today but God broth me out every time he always make away for his children people did me wrong but God kept me strong in my storms and trails and problems those people may get by with me but they will not get by with God, KJB Jeremiah 20 verse 11 But the Lord is with me as a mighty terrible one; therefore my persecutors shall stumble and they shall not prevail; they shall be greatly ashamed; for they shall not prosper; their everlasting confusion shall never be forgotten Psalms 91 He that dwelleth in the secret places of the most high shall abide under the shadow of the almighty verse1 verse 2 I will say of the Lord, he is my refuge and my fortress; my God ; in him will I trust, verse3 surely he shall deliver thee from the snare of the fowler, and from the noisome pestilence verse 4 He shall cover thee with his feathers, and under his wings shall thou trust; his truth shall be thy shield and buckler. Verse 5 Thou shalt not be afraid for the terror by night; nor for the arrow that flieth by day; verse 6 Nor for the pestilence that walketh in darkness; nor for the destruction that wasteth at noonday. Verse 7 a thousand shall fall at thy side and ten thousand at thy right hand; but it shall not come night thee verse 8 only with thine eyes shalt thou behold and see the reward of the wicked. Verse 9 Because thou hast made the Lord, which is my refuge, even the most high, thy habitation; verse 10 There shall no evil befall thee neither shall any plague come high thy dwelling. Verse 11 for he shall give his angels charge over thee, to keep thee in all thy ways. Verse 13 thou shalt tread upon the lion and adder, the young lion and the dragon shalt thou trample under feet. Verse 14 because he hath set his love upon me, therefore will I deliver him; I will set him on high, because he hath known my name. Verse 15 he shall call upon me, and I will answer him; I will be with him in trouble; I will deliver him, and honour him. Verse 16 with long life will I satisfy him, and shew him my salvation. Thus saith the Lord, stand ye in the ways, and see, and ask for the old paths where is the good way, and walk therein KJB Jeremiah 6 verse 16 Be not afraid of their faces; for I am with thee to deliver thee, saith the Lord. KJB Jeremiah 1, verse 8 Be not afraid of their faces; for I am with thee to deliver thee, saith the Lord. Great is my boldness of speech toward you. great is my glorying of you; I am filled with comfort, I am exceeding joyful in all our tribulations. KJB 2 Corinthians 7 verse 4 My goals, is to help others let them know there hope in God his favors never will end.

Jesus will never leave you this far and will never leave you by yourself, Fear not; for I am with thee; KJB Isaiah 43 verse 5 KJB Isaiah 54 verse 4 Fear not; for thou shalt not be ashamed neither be thou confounded; for thou shalt not be put to shame; But God show up for me again, My God always have a solution to my problem when I am going through by reading the bible everyday. when you have God on your side noting is to hard when the master has you in his hand.

My progress in time of need Jesus always got us cover if only you believe and focus on God word and obey and do his will, when God move he does it quickly.

Proverbs 8 verse KJB 34 Blessed is the man that heareth are watching daily at my gates, waiting at the posts of my doors. For whose findeth me findeth life and shall obtain favour of the Lord. Verse 35. Verses 36, But he that sinneth against me wrongth his own soul; all they that hate me love death. For the wages of sin is death; but the gift of God is eternal life through Jesus Christ our Lord. KJB Romans 6 verse 23 threw my days growing up I did not understand to mush about being like Christ like I went to threw a lots of emotions like depressed lonely and could not understand my friends withdraw from me like they did not won't be around me no more, they use to make fun me when I try to tell them about God word, they mock me and make fun of me and use me and hurt me all the time, all threw my life is like bad dream, as growing older I try to spend more time with God by looking for him daily in my everyday life, it was not easy I keep failing but God kept picking back up again, I keep messing up all of time but God cover me by grace because I look for God and listen to him in my daily life and he was outside at the gates 24 hours day every day of my life if I would not looking for God and kept doing what I was doing I would been injure myself like the world who hate God. I would been dead

By praying and searching the bible studying and obey the will of God and singing I would not be here, And now dear brothers and sisters, one final thing. Fix your thoughts on what is true, and honorable, and right, and pure, and lovely, and admirable. Think about things that are excellent and worthy of praise, keep putting into practice all you learned and received from me everything you heard from me and saw me doing, Then the God of peace will be with you. KJB Philippians' 4 verse 8-9 in the word of God also says, finally, brethren, whatsoever things are true, whatsoever things are honest, whatsoever things are just. whatsoever things are pure, whatsoever things are lovely, whatsoever things are of good report; if there be any virtue, and if there be any praise think on these things, Those things, which ye have both learned. And received. And heard, and seen in me do; and the God of peace shall be with you. But I rejoice in the Lord always when I'm going through, He's able and He never fail me yet. KJB things are just whatsoever things are pure, whatsoever things are and there is no sin in him, anyone who continues to live in him will not Whosoever committeth sin transgresseth also the law; for sin is the transgression of law. Verse 5 And ye know that he was manifested to take away our sins; and in him is no sin. Verse 6 Whosoever sinneth hath not seen him, neither known him. Verse 7 Little children, let no man deceive you; he that doeth righteousness is righteous, even as he is righteous. KJB 1John 3 verse 4-5-6-7 KJB Jeremiah 32 verse Behold, I am the Lord the God of flesh; is there any thing too hard for me? is not easy being a christen but God is still in control of my trials in my life every day. My Lord got me cover each step of my storms he allways been so good all of the time. he always show up for me every time all threw my life God show up for me he never let me down. He say do not fear I am your God. In the Lord put I my trust; how say ye to my soul, flee as a bird to your mountain? Verse 2 For. Lo, the wicked bend their bow. They make ready their arrow upon the string, that they may privily shoot at the upright in heart. If the foundations be destroyed, what can the righteous do? Verse 4 The Lord is in his holy temple, the Lord's throne is in heaven; his eyes behold, his eyelids try, the children of men. Verse 5 The Lord trieth the righteous; but the wicked and him that loveth violence his soul hateth. Verse 6 upon the wicked he shall rain snares, fire and brimstone and an horrible tempest; this shall be the portion of their cup. Verse 7 for the righteous Lord loveth righteousness; his countenance doth behold the upright. KJB Psalm 11verse 3-4-5-6-7 I am on the Road of recovery of depression my mind was all mess up I had to be put in the mental hospitals because my thoughts was not right I want to get help so my mom and dad had me put in the hospital for a on none disorders

In 11 1993 of August, I was so mess up I count not act the same I use to act being in my right mine. I was not the same frame of mine as I were use too. So went for help so my mom and dad took to the mental hospitals my dad had to fill the papers out for me because I could not stable at the time. So I stay there for week that first night I was there I reach out to the Lord that night I Knew God was in my life and on my side I pray and cry out to him people try to stop me but no one will stop me from going to my Jesus, he inner seed to the father for me that night For Zion's sake will I not hold my peace, and for Jerusalem's sake I will not forth as brightness, and the salvation thereof as a lamp that burneth. KJB Isaiah 62 verse 1 He sent from above, he took me; he drew me out of many waters; he delivered me from my strong enemy, and from them that hated me; for they were too strong for me. They prevented me in the day of my calamity; but the Lord was my stay. He brought me forth also into a Large place; he delivered me, because he delighted in me. The Lord rewarded me according to my righteousness; according to the cleanness of my hands hath he recompensed me. Verse 22 For I have kept the ways of the Lord. And have not wickedly departed from my God. Verse 23 for all his judgments were before me; and as for his statutes, I did not departed from them. Verse 25 I was also upright before him, and have kept myself from mine iniquity. KJB 2Samuel 22 verse 17-18-19-20-22-23-24-25 Praying and praising the Lord all night and reading and obeying God that's my only my desire to spent time with Jesus he save me by grace I was so happy in Christ that's life Jesus saith unto him, I am the way, the truth, and the life; no man cometh unto the Father but by me. KJB John 14 verse 6 he said to them, Victory we got the Victory was won in Christ Jesus, in the morning his mercy new every morning' my family were very supported they visited me and pray for me my mom and dad visit me and my grandma and a lady pastor my mom ask her to come to see me and pray for me as well, verse 8 I have set the Lord always before me; because he is at my right hand. I shall not be moved. verse 9 Therefore my heart is glad, and my glory rejoiceth; my flesh also shall rest in hope. Verse 10 For thou wilt not leave my soul in hell; neither wilt thou suffer thine holy one to see corruption. Verse 11 Thou wilt shew me the path of life; in thy presence is fullness of joy; at thy right hand there are pleasures for evermore. KJB Psalm 16 in one of the verse. When you mark for a blessing, the wicked know this, so do everything they can to try to stop you but God got you cover when they try to curse you but God steps in every time and when you blow it. when God on your side you cannot lose, No weapon that is formed against thee shall prosper KJB Isaiah54 verse17 When I weak God is strong I get closer to God he make me strong He helps me to be a better person when I go through storms. my God go of head of me to fight my battles, No matter what come your way God have my life in his hands, I know I under God's protected custody For I know the thoughts that I think toward you, saith the Lord. Thought of peace, and not of evil, to give you an expected end then shall ye call upon me, and ye shall go and pray unto me I will hearken unto you. KJB Jeremiah 29 verses 11-12.

Hope. To hope with basis is bible verses from scriptures I know there is a hope air with Christ Jesus he provides Health opportunity for people everywhere Expectation of fulfillment that's success a cure from the Lord himself, now that's a desire accompanied for victory I chosen you and will not throw you away KJB Isaiah 41 verse 9 Thou whom I have taken from the ends of the earth, and called thee from the chief men thereof, and said unto thee, thou art my servant; I have chosen thee, and not cast thee away. Then the word of the Lord came unto me, saying, before I formed thee in the belly I knew thee; and before thou camest forth out of the womb I knew thee; and I ordained thee a prophet unto the nations. KJB Jeremiah 1 verse 4-5 is important that God no us and we know him without Jesus I would be lost, so I try to seek him daily every day of my life he chose the lost and the lest and the dumb to be is display someday my God will make my name as famous as anyone who has lived on earth, someday his will be done. Ye are of God, little children, and have overcome them; because greater is he that is in you, than he that is in you, than he that is in the world. KJB 1John 4 verse 4 God always show up for me when I was growing up and all threw my life he even show for me even I did not show up for him, But God he save me by his grace, when the wicked come in to try pull me in for destruction God steps in every time. They thought I was so stupid because I did not speak up or fight for myself. They try to set me up every time I look around, one of the women I use work with call herself try to set me up on my job they lie said I was a deaf that I took something and one of the manger at the time Lucy she had the people on the job to move are cars on other side of the parking lot all of us and she thought it was good plain Lucy talk it over to the security department she was thinking is was a master mine plan to get me fired, noting. but God is still in control my God had me cover from her dirty plan back fire on her and she look dumb she was shame and she feel stupid, I know my God got me cover he keep me safe and all circumstance because I keep union with Christ Jesus, Blessed are they which are they which are persecuted for righteousness sake; for theirs is the kingdom of heaven. Blessed are ye, when men shall revile you, and persecute you, and shall say all manner of evil against you falsely, for my sake. KJB Matthew 5 verse 10-11 Behold, I have graven thee upon the palms of my hands; thy walls are continually before me. KJB Isaiah 49 verse 16 for there is trouble Jesus is there on the Double. God is not a man, that he should lie; neither the son of man, that he should repent; hath he said, and shall he not do it? Or hath he spoken, and shall he not make it good? Verse 20 behold, I have received commandment to bless; and he hath blessed; and I cannot reverse it, verse 21He hath not beheld iniquity in Jacob, neither hath he seen perverseness in Israel; the Lord his God is with him, and the shout of a king is among them. KJB Numbers 23 verse 19 threw 21 Continue to treat others with Love, no Matter how bad they hurt you, when going through conflict with others people when they wrong doers and put you and pain and they broke your heart, Take it to the lord in prayer always even when we are wrong sometimes pray to Jesus no matter how they may hurt you are to take it to the lord in prayer to help you to forgive others and pray to God to forgive you to. Therefore I say unto you, what things soever ye desire, when ye pray, believe that ye receive them, and ye shall have them. And when ye stand praying, forgive, if ye have ought against any; that your Father also which is in heaven may forgive you your trespasses. KJB Mark 11 verse 24-25 I was going through all kinds problem in my life people hurt me in every wrong doing in but god always had me cover all of the time. I was angry and bitter and broken in bleeding and took vengeance on people but I no deep inside I admit I was wrong and all kinds of trouble came my ways. I repent to God over and over again and apology to God every day of my life I did not give up on Jesus and Jesus did not give up on me I know God was real and know he love me, It took process But I did not give up on my Lord I knew He would show up for me every time. KJB Job 10 verse 12 Thou hast granted me life and favour, and thy visitation hath preserved my spirit. God always answer my prayer and every circumstances, time want by Lost my Grand mom in 202 and my mom and 204 I told her I love her and did real lice it would be her last time I see her, I got the news the last minute she passed away in 204 in the evening in April she and my dad went to my cozen birthday party that even and she got very ill and she had to be rush to the Emergency room My brother came to my home he woke me up in the middle of the night because he could not get hole of me on the phone because I was in a deep sleep. Paul had a key to my house for an emergency purposes he told me is Mom she very sick she in the E, R. we got to get there right away so I got MY self together and we drove to the E,R, When Paul and got there Kennedy Greg wife and my knees and nephew were little at the time and my cozen Lisa and Greg and my Dad and my pastor Jim were there. When I open the door to mom room, I said How is she doing Lisa my cozen who had the Birthday party said She said my mom was gone I hit the floor crying out with tears in my eyes my brother Greg could believe it he rush out the E,R, with on believe with tear in his eyes he ran out in his car and drove away Paul my other brother cry as well Even we all could not believe my mom was gone forever my dad he very sad also.

It was the hardest day of my life the wait and faunal came and went. My family and I went through a storm that day, my Family and my church friends game out to support us and giving us Sympathy cards and prayer. And lets us know they care as from my pastor as well. Everything changed noting stay the same in the monument of time we have to expect what may come are way, But God had us cover every step of the way in are journey. As we approach life Responded even when is good or bad because God is in control, KJB Ecclesiastes 3 verse 1 to everything there is a season, and a time to every purpose under the heaven; Verse 2 A time to be born, and a time to die; a time to plant, and a time to pluck up that which is planted; Verse 3 A time to kill, and a time to heal; a time to break down, and a time to build up; Verse 4 A time to weep, and a time to laugh; a time to mourn, and a time to dance; Verse 5 A time to cast away stones, and a time to gather stones together; a time to embrace, and a time to refrain from embracing; Verse 6 A time to get, and a time to lose; a time to keep, and a time to cast away; Verse 7 A time to rend, and a time to sew; a time to keep silence, and a time to speak; Verse 8 A time to love, and a time to hate; a time of war, and a time of peace. Verse 14 I know that, whatsoever God doeth, if shall be for ever; no-thing can be put to it, nor any thing taken from it; and God doeth it, that men should fear before him. verse 15 That which hath been is now; and that which is to be hath already been; and God reqireth that which is past. Now as I read my daily word God always has an answer for my circumstances on days when I go through storms

I pray and read my bible scripture on my journey every day of my life. Jesus is restoring me and renewing my mine he let us know he recognize are problems he got everything under control I have spoken it, I will also bring it to pass; I have purposed it, I will do it. KJB Isaiah 46-11 As I approach A new day God a has a plane for me and courage words to look forward To I Praise God anyhow I know my future Looks great with God on my side things will suddenly change for me and my Family. A little one shall become a thousand and a small one a strong nation; I the Lord will hasten it in his time. KJB Isaiah 60 verse 22

Year 206 KJB Jeremiah 33 verse 9-11 And it shall be to me a name of joy, a praise and an honour before all the nation of earth, which shall hear all the good that I do unto them; and they shall fear and tremble for all the goodness and for all the prosperity that I procure unto it. The voice of joy, and the voice of gladness, and the voice of the bridegroom, and the voice of the bride, the voice of them that shall say, praise the Lord of hosts; for the Lord is good; for his mercy endureth for ever; and of them that shall bring the sacrifice of praise into the house of the Lord. I going through all kind depressing in my life But I still trust Jesus in my everyday life I still fellowship with God on my regular bases. On my job the mangers gave me a hard time and I still was going thought and still thanking of

My Mother pasting and Grandma as well but God still had his hand on me and let me know everything going work according to his will. and things got worse I lost my Job and I was broke and no income what so ever But I still trust God I kept on seeking him with all my heart I did give up on God and he still did not give up on me. Oh Lord I Acknowledged your Name. What you done for me today, I am alive and well and I still have confident in you o Lord thank you Jesus you always fulfilled your will, and you and very helpful my hope is in you oh Lord I proud to be your child,

Psalm KJB 31 verse 19 Oh how great is thy goodness, which thou hast laid up for them that fear thee; which thou hast wrought for them that trust in thee before the sons of men!

Renee book

Before talking about the word we need to read the guidance of God's word and are everyday life, KJB Psalm 48 verse 14 For this God is our God for ever and ever; he will be our guide ever; unto death, whether in my bad days I made a decision to have a spiritual walk with Jesus to develop a guide to changed how live according to God's will thought hard times facing struggle and circumstances in my life Journey my Hope is in God, he is the only help I know who always keeps his promises he never fell me yet Regardless what going on I will succeed all my goals in Life. But they that wait upon the Lord shall renew their strength; they shall mount up with wings as eagles; they shall run and not be weary and they shall walk, and not faint. KJB Isaiah 40 verse 31 My Lord has Favor on me he persevere me before the foundation of the word I had lots of battle in my life But God had me cover every step of the way Even I was not walking right some days or not obeying God like I should But God is helping me each step every day of my life, Even today he my spiritual guide coach coaching me and the right Directions, KJB Genesis 28 verse 15 and behold I am with thee and will keep in all places whither thou goest, Jesus is my Leader I will obey his commands and be delight in his teaching and his directions to way to go as he spoke the word of God in every generation still yet to come. Look for the Rainbow why you are outside, Possibility will take time on God's timing not on are time But the Lord time we will recede hope from God promises when not looking for are break through that's are surprise just like one your friends throw you a party and when you walk in the room when you not looking when you turn on the lights and all of that moment everything change and right in front of you, and you being praying and wishing for that birthday party surprise you want it for years but no one had the resource to plan the surprise birthday party and you finely forget and think no more about it and that day God Remembrances because you trust and Pray and let it go And God already took care of the production and had already schedule the appointment suddenly your whole life circumstances is a new beginning for your life, KJB Jeremiah 31-17 And there is hope in thine end saith the Lord When take to the Lord in prayer and let it go of your breakthrough regardless how long it may take place keep praying until God answer your prayer things will changed overnight it will happened. When you have an Assignment God not gone lets you miss your positions your Appointment is already on schedule God got you on his report before you even call he already answer your prayer, Then shall ye call upon me, and ye shall go and pray unto me, and I will hearken unto you. KJB Jeremiah 29 verse12-1 Mental Health Recovery, all my life I been going through mental illness shy uncomfortable Very Emotions all of time worried and feeling bad down but not out by Education myself by going to mental health programs to help other to let them know there is hope in God out there if I can get well they can too I would like to be an Leadership someday by supporting the community to let them know there help out there when you going through mental Problems, People with Disabilities are people to they are Human being are going through bad times too and they can make a comeback to others are going through as well with provided meds for your health and seeing your doctor on Regular basis you will be ok. By doing are part we can make progress, I am recovery from Schizophrenic I had for 20 years, I doing much better stronger and wiser and God give me the strength today and every day of my life I have a lots of support other people and my family as well with love and kindness now I doing good Now keep myself in ministries in the missing fill and take time to help others when I go through every day, I take one step of the time each day on my journey on my everyday life, I spin more time with God well try too. I have a positive attitude about myself I believe God and his will for my life should be fulfilled faith in my Lord by study the word of God and practicing in his present helps my progress by keeping me strong when I weak Praying is the main key of Life especially on my bad days and when going through miserable problem and emotions hurting even I don't understand but I Still trust God my promotion will take place one day the glory of God answer a coming change already been spoken KJB Isaiah 30 verse 21 And thine ears shall hear a word behind thee, saying, this is the way, walk ye in it, when ye turn to the right hand. And when ye turn to the left. KJB Romans 3 verse 23 For all have sinned, and come short of the glory of God; verse 24 Being justified freely by his grace through the redemption that is in Christ Jesus; KJB Mark 9 verse 1 and he said unto them, verily I say unto you, that there be some of them that stand here, which shall not taste of death till they have seen the kingdom of God come with power. KJB Revelation 22 verse 12 And, behold. I come quickly; and my reward is with me, to give every man according as his work shall be. verse I am Alpha and Omega, the beginning and the end, the first and the last. 13 I am Looking forward for a brighter future but I believe what I Receive When I have good memories What God did for me I praise the lord anyhow KJB James 1 verse 5 if any of lack wisdom, let him ask of God, that giveth to all men liberally. And upbraideth not; and it shall be given him. The Love of God By a pastor the love of God is with you in grace and peace in time of trouble and turmoil remember nothing can separate us from the love of God-this is peace in the midst of the storm, KJB Psalm 46 verse 19 For this God is our God for ever and ever; he will be our guide even unto death. KJB Psalm 119 verse 105 Thy word is a lamp unto my feet, and a light unto my path. KJB Joshua 1 verse 5 There shall not any man be able to stand before thee all the days of thy life; as I was with Moses, so I will be with thee; I will not fail thee, nor forsake thee. Verse 8 This book of the law shall not depart out of thy mouth; but thou shall meditate therein day and night, that thou mayest observe to do according to all that is written therein; for then therein; for then thou shall make thy way prosperous, and then thou shalt have good success. My God keeps his word when he said it, it should be done, The Lord is very good to me on my journey today he bless my plans to be perfect all through the day and he's not gone leave this far and leave me by myself now. He has everything under control I will not quit on my Lord and Jesus will not quit on me. So why do I complain or worried because God will be there quick fast and an hurry So I thank carefully and positive when I going through struggle I know God will be there on the double and he restore my trouble, is not nice to talk about people when they fell or pick on them when they fall or make fun of others because they are special needs or not if you criticize them it will come back at you of course be on guard what you say about other or you will be hurt by yours own words. Be a help to people you'll have life wealth living for by bean a sample of Christ because you will weep what you sow you will be bless by the best from God KJB Blessed are they which are persecuted for righteousness' sake; for theirs is the kingdom of heaven. Verse 11 Blessed are ye, when men shall revile you, and manner of evil against you falsely, for my sake. Verse 12 Rejoice, and be exceeding glad; for great is your reward in heaven; for so persecuted they the prophets which were before you. Genesis 12 verse 3 And I will bless them that bless thee, and curse him that curseth thee; and in thee shall all families of the earth be blessed. But God will help me every step of the way when I going through storms. I completely give it to God in prayer, when someone do you wrong they do nothing but hurting they self because they the one will fail not you in my past my old guy friend use me even he told me he was using me, he really hurt me Robert Would ask me for sugar and stamps and want a plate of food and envelopes and mansion And money every time he called he won't something almost every day he bug me all of the time most of the day. See he use to lives two doors down from me where I stay. One day I put a stop to that, he told he got married Con to find out he never was devoice he had me to believe he was not married, and Bob got the nerve ask for help again I told him that's not my concern that's you and your wife responsibilities don't come to my house again when you see me just say hi and keep stepping you not welcome here, then days past I kind of new Robert lost everything He want back where he came from back in the dumps what he did to me boomerang right back on him I think he want rock bottom his women friend he was with at the time she made a dummy out of him and kick him to the curve I dump Bob at the time because he wanted to be with Angle so I set him free after he beg me back 3 times to take him back so said ok like a dummy and very same day Robert call Angle right in front of me like I was to Dum asking her to come over his house this we eking, after he got to talking to her I did speak for while then I said to Bob if you want to be with Angle that's fine with me I will never being your Women not now or ever again for now on we just be friends you mess are relationship we will never be no connecting not now or forever even his own wife don't want nothing to do with him that's what he get for trying to get over on people you don't get good come to you when you try get over on somebody, you will get your pay back and he got it too. As look toward the window think of the memories what God brought out today I did say no complaining word out my mouth God show up what had happened I went out today to take care some business and have got done early my ride could not come Wright then A very nice old lady over herd me talk on the phone and she was concern about me getting home she started to talk to me abound her life story and I listen to her and courage her and pray with her about God and telling her don't worried God will take care of you KJB Philippians 4 verse 19 But my God shall supply all your need according to his riches in glory by Christ Jesus. I telling her What the scripture In the bible AND ALLSO God not gone leave you this far and leave you by yourself now Just think what he broth you from in your past you made it then and you will make it now I was saying to her don't worry about God have you cover, I was encourage miss bee think positive toward her future.

KJB Mark 10 verse 27. And Jesus looking upon them saitn, with men it is impossible, but not with God; for with God all things are possible. But I say unto you, love your enemies, bless them that curse you, do good to them that hate you, and pray for them which despitefully use you, and persecute you; That ye may be the children of your Father which is in heaven for he maketh his sun to rise on the evil and on the just and on the unjust, For if ye love them which love you, what reward have ye? Do not even the publicans the same? And if ye salute your brethren only, what do ye more than others? Do not even the publicans so? Be ye therefore perfect, even as your Father which is in heaven is perfect. KJB Matthew 5 44-45-46-47-48 So many storms today I had to spend more time with God my enemies do me so wrong but God keep me strong they had no respect for me what so ever they treat me like an animal like I am an outcast they made my Reputation look bad I know something was said about me by my others enemies with false information. I be glad when the Lord pull the covers off them Jon Frankie Leann and Lucy and Jim and they all they did me wrong and try to still make me look like public disgrace. When I have God on my side I can't lose KJB Isaiah 59 verse 15 Yea, truth faileth; and he that departeth from evil maketh himself a prey; and the Lord saw it, and it displeased him that there was no judgment. Verse 16 And he saw that there was no man, and wondered that there was no intercessor; therefore his arm brought salvation unto him; and his righteousness, it sustained him. Verse 17 For he put on righteousness as breastplate, and an helmet of salvation upon his head; and he put on the garments of vengeance for clothing, and was clad with zeal as a cloke. Verse 18 According to their deeds, accordingly he will repay, fury to his adversaries, recompence to his enemies; to the islands he will repay recompence. Verse 19 So shall they fear the name of the

Lord from the west, and his glory from the rising of the sun. When the enemy shall come in like a flood, the spirit of the Lord shall life up a standard against him. Verse 20 And the Redeemer shall come to Zion, and unto them that turn from transgression in Jacob, saith the Lord. Verse 21 As for me, this my covenant with them, saith the Lord; My spirit that is upon thee, and my words which I have put in thy mouth, shall not depart out of thy mouth, nor out of the mouth of thy seed's seed, saith the Lord, from henceforth and forever. the good bible always provide me good information applies to me and God people who go through storms and whirl wind when are enemies give us a hard time, Nevertheless he saved them for his name's sake that he might make his mighty power to be known. KJB Psalm 106 verse 8 And I will make thee unto this people a fenced brasen wall; and they shall fight against thee, but they shall not prevail against thee; for I am with thee to save thee and to deliver thee, saith the Lord, vers 21 And I will deliver thee out of the hand of the wicked, and I will redeem thee out the hand of the terrible. KJB Jeremiah 15 verse 20-21 KJB Fear them not therefore; for there is nothing covered, that shall not be known. Verse 27 What I tell you in darkness, that speak ye in light; and what ye hear in the ear, that preach ye upon the housetops. KJB Matthews KJB 10 verse 26-27 KJB Isaiah 54 verse 4-17 Verse 17 No weapon that is formed against thee shall prosper; For David speaketh concerning him, I foresaw the Lord always before my face, for he is on my right hand, that I Should not be moved; verse 26 Therefore did my heart rejoice and my tongue was glad; morecover also my flesh shall rest in hope; speaketh KJB Acts 2-25-26 And all these blessing shall KJB Deuteronomy 28 verse 2 And all these blessings shall come on thee, and overtake thee, if thou shalt hearken unto the voice of the Lord thy God. But straightway Jesus spake unto them, saying, be of good cheer; it is I; be not afraid. KJB Matthew 14 verse 27 on my Journey I had to educate myself and make an appointment with God every day of my life by praying and reading the word of God because deep down in me I was not doing right or living right for God I was bitter mad mean and hurt but I still trust Jesus to help me every step of the way., When I Said, my foot slippeth; thy mercy, O Lord, help me up, KJB Psalm 94-18 Oh Lord help me please give me the strength, I would say it my on my daily regularly basics', I look at the sky and a Rainbow is in the air That God letting me no he keeps his promise for me There is hope in God. Every time I see that Rainbow in that sky I know God keeps his covenant. And it shall come to pass, when I bring a bow shall be seen in the cloud; And I will remember my covenant, which is between me and you and every living creature of all flesh; and the waters shall no more become a flood to destroy all flesh. Verse 16 And the bow shall be in the cloud; and I will look upon it, that I may remember the everlasting covenant between God and every living creature of all flesh that is upon the earth, KJB Genesis 8 verse 14-15 I am a Believer please here me what I have to say and listen, I am telling the honest true this what my God did I cry out to him and he look and heard me and recue me and put out the river of death my mouth, sang to the Lord and he heard my prayer. God is our refuge and strength, a very present help in trouble. Therefore will not we fear, though the earth be removed, and though the mountains be carried into the midst of the sea; KJB Psalm 46 verse 1 if was flirting with evil my Lord would not answer me but he look and pull out of trouble. He heard my prayer, Blessed be God he didn't turn a deaf ear, he stayed with me, loyal in his love, KJB Luke 4 verse 43 And he said unto them, I must preach the kingdom of God to other cities also; for therefore am I sent verse 44 And he preached in the synagogues of Galilee. I had a good day today when I go out front of the public in the community were there different programs I get to Share the gospel about Christ by the way I act with love and kindness and supporting them when they are going through decision on their recovery from different season threw life, In my church outreach hospital and family and others are in need of help that my assignment to educated other people let them there a hope and a chance and a season that God has an appointment time for my day for a breakthrough for me you had to been through to help others where they are going through right now. God is able to take care of you his love will never end. KJB Romans 8 verse 38-39 This is what the Lord says For I am persuaded, that neither death, nor life, nor angels, nor principalities, nor powers, nor things present, nor things to come, Nor height, nor depth, nor any other creature, shall be able to separate us from the love of God, which is in

Christ Jesus our Lord. your Redeemer, the Holy one of Israel, I am the Lord your God who teaches you what is good for you and leads you along the paths you should follow Can a woman forget her sucking child that she should not have compassion on the son of her womb? Yea, they may forget yet will I not forget thee. Behold, I have graven thee upon the palms of my hands; thy walls are continually before me. Lift up thine eyes round about, and behold; all these gather themselves together, and come to thee. As I live, saith the Lord, thou shalt surely clothe thee with them all, as with an ornament and bind them on thee, as a bride doeth. KJB Isaiah 49 verse 15-16-`18 This is what the sovereign Thus saith the Lord God, behold, I will lift up mine hand to the Gentiles, and set up my standard to the people; and they shall bring thy sons in their arms, and thy daughters shall be carried upon their shoulders. And kings shall be thy nursing fathers, and their queens thy nursing mothers; they shall bow down to thee with their face toward the earth, and lick up the dust of thy feet; and thou shalt know that I am the Lord; for they shall not be ashamed that wait for me. VERSE 3 For I am the Lord thy God, the holy one of Israel, thy savior; I gave Egypt for thy ransom, Ethiopia and seba forthee. Verse 4 Since thou wast precious in my sight, thou hast been honourable, and I have loved thee; therefore will I give men for thee, and people for thy life. Verse 5 Fear not; for I am with thee; I will bring thy seed from the east, and gather thee from the east, and gather thee from the west; KJB Isaiah 43 verse 3-4-5 Regardless what we going through struggle in are everyday circumstances God have a word for us for the day we will succeed will be a possibility hope absolutely chance take place And there is hope in thine end, saith the Lord, KJB Jeremiah 31 verse 16-17 there hope for people with mental illness and other people as well because we have a favor of God on are life are condition will be hill by the promise HE don't lie God is not a man, that he should lie; neither the son of man. That he should repent; hatch he said. And shall he not do it or hath he spoken, and shall he not make it good? Behold I have received commamdment to bless; and he hath not beheld iniqity in Jacob neither hath he seen perverseness in is-rael the lord his God is with him and the shout of a king is among them KJB Numbers 23 verse 19-20 KJB

Isaiah 51 verse Heaken to me, ye that follow after righteousness, ye that seek the Lord; look unto the rock whence ye are hewn, and to the hole of the pit whence ye are digged. Verse 2 Look unto Abraham your Father, and unto Sarah that bare you; for I called him alone, and blessed him, and increased him. Verse 3 For the Lord shall comfort Zion; he will comfort all her waste places; and he will make her wilderness like Eden, and her desert like the garden of the Lord; joy and gladness shall be found therein, thanksgiving, and the voice of melody. but God is still is in control I still press him no matter what happen My God will saved me I have to stay strong by God grace I can make it he will answer my prayer in his time, KJB Isaiah 63 verse 7-8 I will mention the loving-kindnesses of the Lord, and the praises of the Lord, according to all that the Lord hath bestowed on us, and the great goodness toward the house of Israel, which he hath bestowed on them according to the multitude of his lovingkindnesses. Verse 8 For he said, Surely they are my people, children that will not lie; so he was their Saviour. Obey the Lord your God and all these blessings will be yours Deuteronomy 28 KJB verse 1 And it shall come to pass, if thou shalt hearken diligently unto the voice of the Lord thy God, to observe and to all his commandments which I command thee this day. That the Lord thy God will set thee on high above all nations of the earth; if you disobey the Lord your God and do not faithfully keep all his commands and laws that I am giving you today, all these evil things will happen to you verse 15 if we don't obey God And we be unfaithful we will run in all kind bad luck so we must obey God by fasting and praying and going to the Throne of grace by reading his word Ye adultererers and adulteresses, know ye not that the friendship of the world is enmity with God? Whosoever therefore will be a friend of the world is the enemy of God. Verse 5 Do ye think that the scripture saith in vain, The spirit that dwelleth in us lusteth to envy? Verse 6 But he giveth more grace. Wherefore he saith, God resisteth the proud, but giveth grace unto the humble. KJB James 4 verse 4-5-6 The Lord knoweth the days of the upright; and their inherit-ance shall be for ever. Psalm KJB 37 verse 18 19 They shall not be ashamed. in the evil time; and in the days of famine they shall be satisfied. Verse 20 But the wicked shall perish. And the enemies of the Lord shall consume; into smoke shall they consume away. KJB Psalm 37 verse 3 Trust in the Lord, and do good; so shalt thou dwell in the land, and verity thou shalt be fed. Delight thyself also in the Lord; and he shall give thee the desires of thine heart. But seek ye first the kingdom of God and his righteousness; and all these things shall be added unto you Matthew KJB 6 verse 33 I have to think positive about life. I am very happy to be here this morning alive and well my God came through for me again he woke me up and start my day fresh, I think the lord for a another day thank you Jesus I acknowledged your name with a hard of thanksgiving I thankful for a new hope and your grace for the day I thank you o Lord for a great day, help me to have patient and have a peace in the Love of Christ in me and my family as well, help us not to give up in throw in the towel. I know we will still win the victory because we got you Jesus on are side I am glad you chose us to be your servants we not perfect but we serve a perfect God. KJB Psalm 41 verse 12 And as for me, thou uphold est me before thy face for ever. verse 13 Blessed be the Lord God of Israel from everlasting, and to everlasting. Amen, and amen. KJB Isaiah 40 verse 31 But they that wait upon the Lord shall renew their strength; they shall mount up with wings as eagles, they shall run, and not be weary; and they shall walk, and not faint. KJB Lamentations 3 They are new every morning; great is thy faithfulness. The Lord is my portion, saith my soul; therefore will I hope in him. The Lord is good unto them that wait for him, to the soul that seeketh him. verse23-24-25 For the Lord will not cast off for ever; verse 31 verse 33 For he doth not afflict willingly nor grieve the children of men. KJB Lamentations 3 verse 40 Let us search and try our ways, and turn again to the Lord. Verse 41 Let us life up our heart with our hands unto God in the heavens. Verse 55 I called upon thy name, o Lord, out of the low dungeon. Verse 56 Thou hast heard my voice; hide not thine ear at my breathing, at my cry. Verse 57 Thou drewest near in the day that I called upon thee; thou sadist, fear not. Verse 58 O Lord, thou hast pleaded the causes of my soul; thou hast redeemed my life. Verse 59 O Lord, thou hast seen my wrong; judge thou my cause. Verse 64 Rendern unto them a recompence, O Lord, according to the work of their hands. Give them sorrow of heart, thy curse unto them. In anger from under the heavens of the Lord. KJB Luke 6 verse 35 But love ye your enemies, and do good and lend, hoping for nothing again; and your reward shall be great, and ye shall be the children of the highest; for he is kind unto the unthankful and evil. Jesus is the only way to live by pay attention to God not your problems take it to the Lord in prayer keep your mine on Christ by reading the word of God or sharing Jesus with other unbelievers who need or want are help some will not receive what you say about God word here what God says and whosoever shall not receive you, nor hear your words, when ye depart out of that house or city, shake off the dust of your feet. KJB Matthew 10 verse 14 And Je'-sus came and spake unto them, saying All power is given unto me in heaven and in earth. Go ye therefore, and teach all nations, baptizing them in the name of the Father, and of the son, and of the Holy Ghost; Teaching them to observe all things, whatsoever I have commanded you; and I am with you always, even unto the end of the world A-men. Matthew KJB 28 verse 18-19-20 Don't being around bad people who do wrong that not nice to do what they do is dead giveaway they will have you all mess up your live will never be the same you will always have trouble in your house hold you will never get it out My son, if sinners entice thee consent thou not. If they say, come with us, let us lurk privily for the innocent without cause; let us swallow them up alive as the grave; and whole, as those that go down into the pit; we shall find all precocious substance, we shall fill our houses with spoil; Cast in thy lot among us; let us all have one purse; My son, walk not thou in the way with them; refrain thy foot from their path; For their feet run to evil, and make haste to shed blood. Surely in vain the net is spread in the sight of any bird. And they lay wait for their own blood; they lurk privily for their own lives. So are the ways of every one that is greedy of gain; which taketh away the life of the owners thereof. KJB Proverbs 1 verse

10-11-12-13-14-15-1617-18-19 That;s not parthership that's War Be ye not unequally yoked together with unbelievers; for what fellowship hath righteousness with unrigheousness? And what communion hath light with darkness. KJB 2 Corinthians 6 verse 14-16 Howbeit when he, the spirit of truth, is come, he will guide you into all truth; for he shall not speak of himself, but whatsoever he shall shew you things to come. He shall glorify me; for he shall receive of mine, and shall shew it unto you. KJB John 16-13 Lord, VERSE. 14 And God also says in the word Love not the world, neither the things that are in the world. If any man love the world, the love of the Father is not in him. For all that is in the world, the lust of the flesh, and the lust of the eyes, and pride of life, is not of the father, but is of the world. And the world passeth away, and the world passeth away, and the lust thereof; but he that doeth the will of God abideth for ever. KJB 1 John 2 verse 15-16-17 But if we walk in the light as he is in the light, we have fellowship one with another, and the blood of Jesus Christ his son cleanseth us from all sin, O taste and see that the Lord is good; blessed is the man that trusteth in him. O fear the Lord, ye his sants; for there is no want to them that fear him. KJB Psalm 34 verse 8-9 Rejoice in the Lord, O ye righteous; for praise is comely for the upright. Praise the Lord with harp; sing unto him with the psaltery and an instrument of ten strings. KJB Psalm 33 verse 4 Blessed be the God and Father of our Lord Jesus Christ.

KJB 1Peter1 verse 3-4-5-6-7-8-9-10-11-12-13-14-15-16-17-18-19-20. Blessed by the best. I all ways say my God did many miracles in my past life he is all some and he is still yet to come he is always on time he may not come when he won't to but he always on time he never fell me yet. I would tell you believe the promise of God and obey his word and everything will stand in place who ever put they trust in God will never be put in shame. I will bless the Lord at all the times and he will give us many benefits and are daily life. Whatever asks and believe him or pleasing in his sight by obeying his will always have abundance life. KJB John 14 verse 13 whatever you ask in my name, that I will do, that the Father may be glorified in the son. Here is one miracle happen to me in year 207 I was coming from the corner store one day in the summer and one my neighbor miss Jane came walking over to me asking me for money I told her I don't have no money what so ever but only food stamps that's all what I have and she was angry at me she start calling me bad names And she hurt me so bad I overcome evil with good kind words to miss Jane even dough I have tears in my eyes crying to myself what did I did wrong but treat her nice in the past I use to give her cookies and candy all of times every time I come from the corner store all the time. As went back to my apartment crying to the Lord on my knees saying have mercy on her soul I pray to God out loud for Miss Jane and pray for the best for her. And time would past and one day she came to me and told me she was sorry and said you never done know harm to me and she gave a hung and she made her peace with me and she never was mean to me again. And a another incident my friend and I went to a burger restaurant to eat on a winter day of the year 208 I went to the Lady restroom and I was very nice to this Lady I just ask her question she came at me cussing me out and wanted to hurt me and I said the Lord is internal forever

I said to her about Four or five times and by the grace of God I was out the rest room I did know how is was but God. And lots of people at the rest room was shook and my friend Debbie knew her and said Renee don't say a word and come to find out Debbie is the one who give her food sometimes when she need it. So Debbie knew who she was and that lady who did me wrong was so shame she walk out the restaurant and never came back again. Psalm 12-7-8 KJB The Lord shall preserve you from all evil; he shall preserve your soul. The Lord shall preserve your going out and your coming in from time, and even forth, and even forevermore.

By Grace I am save because by obeying Jesus which is the only way to do when I am going through all Circumstances But Still I Trust God in my trouble my example being connect to a Relationship with God means give my all to him I don't always worship like I should but I will try to go back to my daily visited to reached the throne of mercy and grace He answered and said unto them, because it is given unto you to know the mysteries of the kingdom of heaven, but to them it is not given. For whosoever hath, to him shall be given, and he shall have more abundance; but whosoever hath not, from him shall be taken away even that he hath. Verse 13 Therefore speak I seeing see not; and hearing they hear not, neither do they understand. Verse 14 And in them is fulfilled the prophecy of Esai as, which saith, By hearing ye shall hear, and shall not understand; and seeing ye shall see, and shall not perceive; verse For this people's heart is waxed gross. And their ears are dull of hearing, and their eyes they have closed; lest at any time they should see with their eyes and hear with their ears. And should understand with their heart, and should be converted, and I should heal them. Verse 16 But blessed are your eyes, for they hear. Verse 17 For verily I say unto you, That many prophets and righteous men have desired to see those things which ye hear, and have not heard them. Verse18 Hear ye therefore the parable of the sower. Verse 19 When any one heareth the word of the kingdom, and understandeth it not, then cometh the wicked one, and catcheth away that which was sown in his heart. This is he which received seed by the way seed by the way side. Verse 20 But he that received the seed into stony places, the same is he that heareth the word, and anon with joy receiveth it; verse 21 Yet hath he not root in himself, but dureth for a while; for when tribulation or persecution ariseth because because of the word, by and by he is offended. Verse 22 He also that received seed among the thorns is he that heareth the word; and the care of this world, and the deceitfulness of riches choke the word, in becometh unfruitful. Verse 23 But he that received seed into he good ground is he that heareth the word, and understandteth it; which also beareth fruit, and bringeth forth, some an hundredfold, some sixty, some thirty. KJB Matthew 13 verse 11 12-13-14 threw20-21-22-23 Those who wait on the Lord shall renew their strength; they shall mount up with wings like eagles, they shall run and not be weary, they shall walk and not faint. Isaiah 40 verse 31 KJB Romans 15 verse 4-5Whatever things were written aforetime were written for our learning that we through patience and comfort of the scriptures might have hope. Now may the God of patience and comfort grant you to be like-minded toward one another, according to Christ Jesus are you listen to God he speaking to you obey and here what he saying to you The eternal God is your refuge. And underneath are the everlasting arms; he will thrust out the enemy from before you, and will say. Destroy!'Deuteromy 33verse 27 KJB STEPT 1 you must have a relationship with God in your prayer life. Important to always walk with God at all time's listen Jesus will respond oh Lord help me to pay attention and worship you. STEPT 2 Obeying God is the main key is better than sacrifice. Step3 fast and pray and walk in the narrow way. KJB Romans 12 verse 1 I beseech you therefore brethren. By the mercies of God, that ye present your bodies a living sacrifice holy, acceptable unto God, which is your reasonable service. Verse 2 and be not conformed to this world; but be ye transformed by the renewing of your mind, that ye may prove what is that good, and acceptable. And perfect, will of God. Step4 KJB Deuteronomy 10 verse 12 And now Israel, what doth the Lord thy God require of thee but to fear the Lord thy God, to walk in all his ways and to love him, and to serve his ways. And to love him. And to serve the Lord thy God with all thy heart and with all thy soul, Step 5 KJB Matthew 6 verse 24 KJB. No man can serve two masters; for either he will hate the one, and love the other, or else he will hold to the one, and despise the other, Ye cannot serve God and mannon. fear not, for I am with you; be not dismayed, for I am your God. I will strengthen you, Yes, I will help you. I will uphold you with my righteous right hand. Isaiah 41 VERSE 10 KJB Believe in the possible.

Always in every prayer of mine for you all making request with joy, verse 5 for your fellowship in the gospel from the first day until now, verse 6 being confident of this very thing, that he which hatch begun a good work in you will perform it until the day of Jesus Christ, is by stating now to have fellowship with God ask Jesus in life right now he take you as you are repent. Ask God in your life and save me for Jesus sake and asks the Lord what to do. Regardless what going on in your life ether you have a bad day or good days even you don't understand obey and trust Jesus in your journey everyday life. KJB Mark 10 verse 27 And Jesus looking upon them sath, with God; all things are possible. Psalm 46 verse 1KJB God said in his word God is our refuge and strength, a very present help in trouble.

Wait on God. To take care of the circumstances Progress has all been providing without delay God have you cover you. You are bless by the best. Genesis 18 KJB verse 14 is any thing too hard for the Lord? Proverbs 8 KJB verse 34 blessed is the man that heareth me watching daily at my gates. Wating at the hosts of my doors. Verse 35 But he that sinneth against me wrongeth his own soul; all they that hate me love death. John 12 verse 46 I am come a light into the world. That whosoever believeth on me should not abide in darkness. Verse 47 and if any man hear my words and believe not, I judge him not; for I came not to judge the world. But to save the world. Verse 48 He that rejecteth me, and recived not my words, hath one that I have spoken, the same shall judge him in the last day. verse 49 for I have not spoken of myself; be the Father, which sent me, he gave me a commandment. What I should say, and what I should speak. My journey for the day God is precious to me he will be always my first love in my life KJB Psalms 36 verse 7 How excellent is thy lovingkindness, God! Therefore the children of men put their trust under the shadow of thy wings. Verse 8 They shall be abundantly satisfied with the fatness of thy house; and thou shalt make them drink of the river of thy pleasures.

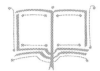

Today was a great day Everything thing work out according to God's plan I had my good days and my bad days But God Response to my prayer Every chance he get when I call on God he answer Psalm 91 KJB verse 15 He shall call upon me. And I will answer him; I will be with him in trouble, I will deliver him, and honour him verse 16 With long life will I satisfy him, and shew him my salvation. KJB Psalm 63 verse 1-5 O God, You are my God; Early will I seek you; My soul thirsts for you; my flesh longs for you . . . so I have looked for you in the sanctuary, to see your power and your glory. Because your lovingkindness is better is better than life, my lips shall praise you. Thus I will bless you while I live; I will life up my hands in your name. my soul shall be satisfied as with marrow and fatness, and my mouth shall praise you with joyful lips. I was going through all kind of troubles but God had me cover by his grace he Established it before the foundation of the world, my enemies try to put all kind of interruption they try to trap me But God show for me every time. KJB Psalm 91 verse 1 he that dwelleth in the secret place of the most high shall abide under the shadow of the almighty. Verse 2 I will say of the Lord he is my refuge and my fortress; my God; in him will I trust. When I was going up. This Lady my mom friend She was so funny she and her husband name was miss Bobbie Ann and Mister Jackson they both was Laughable so funny in a nice kind of way miss Bobbie Ann would chew her gum all day every day until the point my brother Paul. Was nine at the time ask her do you sleep with your gum. One time my Mother and miss Bobbie Ann went ridding on an ornery day and my mom seen too big garbage cans in the middle of the street and my mom drive around them and miss Bobbie Ann said Darlene why you going around for my mom said Bobbie Ann did you see that too big garbage cans in the street No I did even see those garbage cans I would had too cans, dragging under my car and my mom laugh so hard and told are family about, and the other time she fell in the hall closet over my family house when my dad was there at the time when the Jackson was over there for a visit that day see we had a walk in closet Bobbie Ann were talking and for she no It she fell right in the closet I thought was funny to myself MY dad was trying not to laugh so was daddy friend Bill came to visit too. Mister Jackson pick her up ASK Her if she ok and all of us were concern about her wellbeing but deep down inside we was had lots laughers to miss Bobbie Ann was not hurt at all Thank God for that, that's was 1984 back in the days was fun times when my cozen Toni was riding with us and we went over the miss Bobbie Ann house my mom told her don't stare at her she real funny she very laughable she will make you crack up Miss Bobbie Ann chewing her gum and talking very funny Toni was looking real close she was almost in her lap looking at her face with laugher. My mom said I told you she is very funny to be around, This is a very funny story Once upon time miss Bobbie Ann was sitting home watching television at night while her husbands was at work she heard someone at her door she thought it was her son James she said James is that you she open the door all of a sudden she finely knew that was not her son James she look down the man did not have no pants on or shirt ether he just had a jacket on in flash her and Bobbie Ann slam the door and lock it and shout out loud and she made called to Master Jackson her husband she said Jackson A naked man was at the door he said don't call me Bobbie Ann called the police. she love my mother cooking she was pitching off the lemon cake my mom made for Bobbie Ann when we was over her house Mister Jackson was on the telephones he told her write down the telephone number and Bobbie Ann was not even listening he look up and said you would not even listing what I was saying I ask you get peace paper and write down a phone number you busy pitching off that cake Darlene made for her. those was the good old days as I sit back and look at my cat Gemini he remind me of old cat Gemini the first he was a very smart cat too smart for his good he would get In lots of trouble one time we brought him so cat food he did like it he would cover it up with his other food pan lets us know he would eat it sometime my brother would go by him some cat food because the cat would starve his self he would eat a hole day unless you by the cat food he like sometimes the cat would bring a chipmunk from outside and run through the house with the chip month in his mouth we had to close all the doors in the house so he would not get in are rooms MY Granma was there to visit and she was there when the cat had chase the chip month all over the house Granma got scared and jump on the top of the chair and finely my brother Lemont hit the chip moth with the broom and everything was over the cat stop and look and he had no need of the chip moth and the chip month was no more, and others times are cat would boss my daddy my mother would tell the cat way until granddaddy come home she says to the cat the cat would get in front of the door and wait for my dad come home and when he came home my dad would sit down and read the newspaper and he would say Gemini the cat Gemini would you doing gemmy the cat would look at the door and start shouting out loud let him know he won't go outside some time my daddy would not listen and go back to the newspaper and the cat would jump up and grab the newspaper out my father hand and throw the newspaper on the flood and pull his paw over it and look at him and he let him know he mean business. One thanksgiving the cat got In the turkey he loves turkey see the cat would get a table scraps of turkey from all of us he from me Greg and my other brother and my mom and dad the cat walk in the room and flap his self-down in the bed he slept for the whole day until turkey time again. one time he wait until all of us went to sleep and the cat has Is way on the top of the stove of and he got in the pot and took the cover off the pot and took that whole turkey out and got on the floor and had a feast on the turkey the next morning mom got up and saw the cat on the floor with are turkey she was not pleased with that cat my mom whip that cat and put him out side for hole day. That's the thanksgiving we never forgot.

I remember one time this man my father try to sponsor A man from AA his name is Gene had a drugs problem real bad and his mom put him out her house he had no place to stay and my dad wanted Gene stay at my house on the sofa that night my mom did not won't mister Gene in the house my mom had put her too sense and are cat spoke something too in cat talk shouting to my dad too we were surprise the cat spoke his words My mom said even the cat did not want him there ether So my mom put him out and Mister Gene had to sleep in the car I what not blame my mom Mister Gene were on drugs, my dad was only try to help but I say my mom did the right thing, God is not the author of confusion but of peace, as in all the churches of the saints, 1Corinthians 14;33 KJB I had a good day I was going through storms but God is still in control I still press him my week was ok by the grace of God he all some to me always he keeps his promise all of the time I went to my daddy house my family and I my baby brother birthday was today he turn 3 years old he from by father second wife we had a good time we had cake and Ice cream my brother had gift we had a good whole time my family am I and an a old friend from school we grown up together back In the days we all had a good time, The love of God is with you in grace and peace in a time of trouble and turmoil remember nothing can separate us from the love of God-this is peace in the midst of the storm, by a pastor And yet the Lord is waiting to be merciful to you. He is ready to take pity on you because he always does what is right happy are those who but their trust in the Lord, and yet the Lord is waiting to be merciful to you. And therefore will the Lord wait that he may be gracious unto you, and therefore will he be exalted. That he may a God of judgment; blessed are all they that wait for him. KJB Isaiah 30 verse 18 before talking about the word we need to read the guidance of God word and everyday life. He will be our guide even to the end for this God is our God for ever unto death. KJB Psalm 48 verse 14 Believe in God no matter how your breakthrough has not come yet but still have a positive attitude seen like you running all over the community try to find a job and the people slamming the door on you for me myself and I been there and done that but still God is amble to help me it is very painful when people hurt you having you believe they will help you but they just playing you along like they for you but really deep down they don't care if you make it or not with Jesus on my side I will make It and I look toward to a brighter future I will take of you Jeremiah, KJB Jeremiah 15 verse 11 The Lord said, Verily it shall be well with thy remnant; verily I will cause the enemy to entreat thee well in the time of evil and in the time of affiction. Exodus 33 KJB verse 14 And he said my presence shall go with thee, and I will give thee rest. KJB John 14 verse 1 Let not your heart be troubled; you believe in God, believe also in me. Wherefore gird up the loins of your mind, be sober, and hope to the end for the grace that is to be brought unto you at the revelation of Jesus Christ; Because it is written, be ye holy; for I am holy. KJB 1Peter 1 verse 13-16 with God on your side thing will sudden change, when people treat you like garbage God turn it out for his good treasure, Now One day my God will make me famous so everybody on the earth will see me. The Lord upholdeth all that fall and raiseth up all those that be bowed down. The eyes of all wait upon thee; and thou givest them their meat in due season. Psalms 145 verse 14.

Yolanda. Before talking about the word we need to read the guidance of God's word and are everyday life, he my guide even to the end whether in my Difficulties. I made a decision to have a spiritual walk with Jesus to develop a guide to changed how live according to God's will thought hard times facing struggle and circumstances in my life Journey my Hope is in God, he is the only help I know who always keeps his promises he never fell me yet Regardless what going on I will succeed all my goals in Life. But they that wait upon the Lord shall renew their strength. They shall mount up with wings as eagles; they shall run and not be weary and they shall walk and not faint, Isaiah 40 verse 31 KJB My Lord has Favor on me he persevere me before the foundation of the word I had lots of battle in my life But God had me cover every step of the way Even I was not walking right some days or not obeying God like I should But God is helping me each step every day of my life, Even today he my spiritual guide coach coaching me and the right Directions, KJB Genesis 28 verse 15 And behold, I am with thee, and will keep thee in all places whither thou goest, and will bring thee again into this land; for I will not leave thee, until I have done that which I have I have done that which I have spoken to thee of. Jesus is my Leader I will obey his commands and be delight in his teaching and his directions to way to go as he spoke the word of God in every generation still yet to come. Look for the Rainbow why you are outside, Possibility will take time on God's time not on are time But the Lord time we will reseed hope from God promises when not looking for are breakthrough that's are surprise just like one your friends throw you a party and when you walk in the room when you not looking when you turn on the lights and all of that moment everything change and right in front of you, and you being praying and wishing for that birthday party surprise you want it for years but no one had the resource to plan the surprise birthday party and you Findlay forget and think no more about it and that day God Remembrance because you trust and Pray and let it go And God already took care of the production and had already schedule the appointment suddenly your whole life circumstances is a new beginning for your life, KJB Jeremiah 31-16-17 And there is hope in thine end. When you going through storms take to the Lord in prayer and let it go of your breakthrough regardless how long it may take place keep praying until God answer your prayer things will not change overnight it will happened. It may tack time but it will happen When you have an Assignment God not gone lets you miss your positions your Appointment is already on schedule God got you on his report before you even call he already answer your prayer, Then shall ye call upon me. and ye shall go and pray unto me, and I will harken unto you. And ye shall seek me, and find me when ye shall search for me with all your heart, Jeremiah KJB 29 verse12-13.

M ental Health Recovery, all my life I been going through mental illness shy uncomfortable Very Emotions all of time worried and feeling bad down but not out by Education myself by going to mental health programs to help other to let them know there is hope in God out there if I can get well they can too I would like to be an Leadership someday by supporting the community to let them know there help out there when you going through mental Problems, People with Disabilities are people to they are Human being are going through bad times too and they can make a difference to others as well with provided Medicine for your health and seeing your doctor on Regular basis you will be ok. By doing are part we can make a diffidence I am recovery from Schizophrenic I had for 20 years, I doing much better stronger and wiser and God give me the strength today and every day of my life I have a lots of support other people and my family as well with love and kindness now I doing good Now keep myself in ministries in the missing fill and take time to help others when I go through every day, I take one step of the time each day on my journey on my everyday life, I spend more time with God well try too I have a positive attitude about myself I believe God and his will for my life should be fulfilled faith in my Lord by study the word of God and practicing in his present helps my progress by keeping me strong when I weak Praying is the main key of Life especially on my bad days and when going through miserable problem and emotions hurting even I don't understand I Still trust God my promotion will take place one day the glory of God answer a coming change already been spoken KJB 2 Corinthians 3 verse 18 But we all with open face beholding as in a glass the glory of the Lord, are changed into the same image from glory, even as by the spirit of the Lord. Romans KJB 3 verse 23 For all have sinned, and come short of the glory of God;

verse 24 Being justified freely by his grace through the redemption that is in Christ Jesus, KJB Psalm 103 verse 10, 12 He has not dealt with us according to our sins, nor punished us according to our iniquities. As far as the east is from the west, so far has he removed our transgressions from us. Revelation KJB 21 verse 12 and behold I come quickly, and my reward is with me to give every man according as his work shall be verse 13 I am Alpha and Omega the beginning and the end the First and the last I am Looking forward for a brighter future but I believe what I Receive When I have good memories What God did for me I praise the lord anyhow, A man hath joy by the answer of his mouth; and a word spoken in due season how good is it! Proverbs KJB 15 verse 2.

The Love of God By A pastor the love of God is with you in grace and peace in time of trouble. and remember nothing can separate us from the love of God-this is peace in the midst of the storm, Genesis KJB 18 verse 14 is Anything too hard for the Lord Mark 12 verse 30 "You shall love the Lord your God with all your heart, with all your soul, with all your mind, and with all your strength." This is the first commandment. KJB Joshua 1 KJB verse 5 there shall not any man be able to stand before thee all the days of thy life; as I was with Moses, so I will be with thee; I will not fail thee, nor forsake thee. Verse 8 This book of the law shall not depart out of thy mouth; but thou shalt meditate therein day and night; that thou mayest observe to do according to all that is written therein; for then thou shalt have good success. 9 Have not I commamded thee? Be strong and of a good courage; be not afraid, neither be thou dismayed; for the Lord thy God is with thee whithersoever thou goest. My God keeps his word when he said it, it should be done, The Lord is very good to me on my journey today he bless my plans to be perfect all through the day and he's not gone leave this far and leave me by my self now. he has everything under control I will not quit on my Lord And Jesus will not quit on me. So why do I complain or worried because God will be there quick fast and an hurry So I thank carefully and positive when I going through struggle I know God will be there on the double and he restore my trouble, Proverbs 3 verse 5-6 KJB Trust in the Lord with all thine heart; and lean not unto thine own understanding. In all thy ways acknowledge him. And he shall direct thy paths. So let the Lord lead you in the right way of living put the past behind you and forecast on the further I would say to others and myself. all my life people treat me like garbage those people came at me like a whirl wind But God will help me every step of the way when I going through storms I completely give it to God in prayer, when someone do you wrong they do nothing but hurting they self because they the one will fail And I will bless them that bless thee; and curse him that curseth thee; and in thee shall all families of the earth be blessed. KJB Genesis 12 verse 3 back in my past my use to be Boyfriend use me even he told me he was using me, he really hurt me Robert Would ask me for surged and stamps and want a plate of food and envelopes and mansion And money every time he called he won't something almost every day he was a pain in the butt, see he lives two doors down from me where I stay. One day I put a stop to that, he told he got married Con to find out he never was devoice he had me to believe he was not married, and Bob got then ask for help again I told him that's not my concern that's you and your wife responsibilities don't come to my house again when you see me just say hi and keep stepping you not welcome here, then days past I heard Robert lost everything He want back where he came from back in the dumps what he did to me boomerang right back on him I heard he want rock bottom his woman friend he was with at the time she made a dumpy out of him and kick him to the curve and he back to jail for stilling I dump Bob at the time because he wanted to be with Stacy so I set him free after he beg me back 3 times to take him back so said ok like a dummy and very same day Robert call Stacy right in front of me like I was too dumb like did not nodes asking her to come over his house this week king, after he got to talking to her I did speak for while then I said to Bob if you want to be with Stacy that's fine with me I will never being your Women not now ever again for now on we just be friends you mess are relationship we will never be no connecting not now or forever even his own wife don't want nothing to do with him that's what he get for trying to get over on people you don't get good come to you when you try get over on somebody, KJB Hebrews 10 verse 30 For we know him that hath said Vengeance belongeth unto me I will recompense, saith the Lord. And again, the Lord shall judge his people verse 31 it is a fearful thing to fall into the hands of the living God. As look toward the window think of the memories what God brought me out today I did say no complaining word out my mouth God show up what had happened I went out today to take care some business and have got done early my ride could not come wright then A very nice old lady over herd me talk on the phone and she was concern about me getting home she started to talk to me abound her life story and I listen to her and courage her and pray with her about God and telling her don't worried God will take care of you KJB Psalms 55 verse 22 Cast thy burden upon the Lord. And he shall sustain thee; he shall never suffer the righteous to be moved. I telling her What the scripture In the bible and also God not gone leave you this far and leave you by yourself now Just think what he brought you from in your past you made it then and you will make it now I was saying to her don't worry about God have you cover, I was very supported to miss bee think positive toward her future.

KJB Mark 10 verse 27 And Jesus looking upon them saith, With men it is impossible, but not with God; for with God all things are possible. But I say unto you. Love your enemies bless them that curse you, do good to them that hate you. And pray for them which despitefully use you. And persecute you; That ye may be the children of your Father which is in heaven; for he maketh his sun to rise on the evil and on the good, and sendeth rain on the just and on the unjust. For if ye love them which love you, what reward have ye? Do not even the publicans the same? And if ye salute your brethren only, what do ye more than others? Do not even the publicans so? Be ye therefore perfect, even as your Father which is in heaven is perfect. Matthew KJB 5 44-45-46-47-48 So many storms today I had to spend more time with God my enemies do me so wrong but God keep me strong they had no respect for me what so ever they treat me like an animal like I am an outcast they made my Reputation look bad I know something was said about me by my others enemies with false information. I be glad when the Lord pull the covers off them Jon Frankie Leann and Lucy and Jim and they did me wrong and try to still make me look like a public disgrace. When I have God on my side I can't lose Isaiah KJB 59 verse 15 Yea, truth faileth; and he that depareth from evil maketh himself a pray; and the Lord saw it, and it displeased him that there was no judgment verse 16 And he saw that there was no man, and wondered that there was no intercessor; therefore his arm brought salvation unto him; and his righteousness, it sustained him, verse 17 for he put on righteousness as a breastplate and an helmet of salvation upon his head; and he put on the garments of vengeance for clothing, and was clad with zeal as a cloke. the good bible always provide me good information Nevertheless he saved them for his name's sake, that he might make his mighty power to be known. KJB Psalm 106 verse 8 And I will make thee unto this people a fenced brasen wall; and they shall fight against thee, for I am with thee to save thee and deliver out of the hand of the wicked, and I will redeem thee out of the hand of terrible. KJB Jeremiah 15 verse 26-27 Fear them not therefore; for there is nothing covered, that shall not be revealed; and hid, that shall not be known. What I tell you in darkness. That speak ye in light; and what ye hear in the ear, that preach ye upon the housetops. Matthew KJB 10 verse 26-27 KJB Isaiah 54 verse 4-17 Fear not; for thou shalt not be ashamed; neither be thou confounded; for thou shalt not be put to shame; No weapon that is formed against thee shall prosper; KJB Psalms 18 verse 2 I will love thee, O Lord is my rock, and my fortress, and my deliverer; my God. My trust is in the Lord he will always help me in all times I will always praise him for he is good and always show up and show off with him I will never be put to shame.

Obeying is better saying yes to God. On my Journey I had to educate myself and make an appointment with God every day of my life by praying and reading the word of God because deep down in me I was not doing right or living right for God I was bitter mad mean and hurt but I still trust Jesus to help me every step of the way., if I say. Walk in love, as Christ also has loved us and given himself for us, an offering and a sacrifice to God for a sweet-smelling aroma. Speaking to one another in psalms and hymns and spiritual songs, singing and making melody in your heart to the Lord . . . for we are members of his body, of his flesh and of his bones. Ephesians 5;2 19, 30 KJB Oh Lord help me please give me the strength, I would say it my on my daily regularly basics, I look at the sky and a Rainbow is in the air That God letting me no he keeps his promise for me There is hope in God. Every time I see that Rainbow in that sky I know God keeps his covenant. And the bow shall be in the cloud; and I will look upon it, that I may remember the everlasting covenant remember the everlasting covenant between God and every living creature of all flesh that is upon the earth. KJB Genesis 8 verse 16-17 All Believers come here and listen, let me tell you what God did for me, I called out to him with my mouth, my tongue shaped the sounds of music, if I had been cozy with evil the Lord would never have listened, But he most surely did listend, But he most surely did listen, he came on the double when he heard my prayer, Blessed be God he didn't turn a deaf ear, he stayed with me, loyal in his love, KJB Luke 4 verse 43 And he said unto them, I must preach the kingdom of God to other cities also; for therefore am I sent, I had a good day today when I go out front of the public in the community were there different programs I get to Shear the gospel about Christ by the way I act with love and kindness and supporting them when they are going through decision on their recovery from different session threw life, In my church outreach hospital and family and others are in need of help that my assignment to educate other people let them know there a hope and a chance and a season that God has an appointment time for are day for a breakthrough you have to been threw to help others where they are going through right now. God is able to take care of you his love will never end. Neither death nor life neither angels nor demons neither the present nor the future nor any powers neither heigh nor depth, nor anything else in all creation will be able to separate us from the love of God that is in Christ Jesus our Lord. Be of good courage, and he shall strengthen your heart, all ye that hope in the Lord. Psalm 31 verse 24 KJB what is good for you and leads you along the paths you should follow But ever if that were possible, I would not forget you. I have written your name on the palms of my hands, As surely as I live says the Lord they will be like jewels or bridal ornaments for you to display Isaiah 49 KJB verse 15-16-`18 Can a woman forget her sucking child, that she should not have compassion on the son of her womb? Yea, they may forget yet will I not forget thee. Verse 16 Behold, I have graven thee upon the palms of my hands; thy walls are continually before me. They children shall make haste; thy destroyers and they that make thee waste shall go forth of thee. Lift up thine eyes round about, and behold; all these gather themselves together, and come to thee. As I live, saith the Lord, thou shalt surely clothe thee with them all as with an ornament, and bind them on thee, as a bride doeth. Thus saith the Lord God, behold, I will lift up mine hand to the Gentiles, and set up my standard to the people; and they shall bring thy sons in their arms, and thy daughters shall be carried upon their shoulders. Verse 22 verse23 And kings shall be thy nursing Fathers, and their queens thy nursing mother; they shall bow down to thee with their face toward the earth, and lick up the dust of thy feet; and thou shalt know that I am the Lord; for they shall not be ashamed that wait for me. His Decisions are always right, KJB Proverbs 16 verse 3 Commit thy works unto the Lord, and thy thoughts shall be established. KJB Isaiah 43 verse 3-4 For I am the Lord thy God, the holy one of Israel, thy Saviour; I gave Egypt for thy ransom, Ethiopia and seba for thee. Since thou wast precious in my sight, thou hast been honour-able, and I give men for thee, and people for life. Regardless what we going through struggle in are everyday circumstances God have a word for us for the day we will succeed will be a possibility hope absolutely chance take place in are future says the Lord. There KJB Romans 5verse 5 And hope maketh not ashamed; because the love of God is shed abroad in our hearts by the holy Ghost which is given unto us. But God commendeth his love toward us, in that, while we were yet sinners, Christ died for us. But now being made free from sin, and become servants to God, ye have your fruit unto holiness, and the end everlasting life, for the wages of sin is death; but the gift of God is eternal life through Jesus Christ our Lord. KJB Romans 6 verse22-23 hope for people with mental illness and other people as well because we have a favor of God on are life are condition will be hill by the promise God is not man, that he should lie; neither the son of man, that he should repent; hath he said, and shall he not do, it? Or hath he spoken, and shall he not make it good. Behold, I have received commanent to bless; and I cannot reverse it. KJB Numbers 23 verse 19-20.

The justice is not right the wicked all ways get by with crime I know God don't like oppression and those pay under the table to these greedy judges and the court they may get by but God will should punished them at his time. He will pushied them if they don't repent and turn from they wicked ways. I hate oppression and crime, He that dwelleth in the seret place of the most high shall abide under the shadow of the Almighty. I will say of the Lord. He is my refuge and my fortress; my God; in him I trust. Surely he shall deliver thee from the noisome pestilence. He shall cover thee with his feathers, and under his wings shalt thou trust; his truth shall be thy shield and buckler. Psalm 91 verse 1-2-3-4 KJB. I going through suffering but God is still is in control I still praise him no matter what happen My God will saved me I have to stay strong by God grace I can make it he will answer my prayer in his time, For he said, Surely they are my people, children that will not lie; so he was their Savior. In all their affliction he was afflicted, and the angel of his presence saved them; in his love and in his pity he redeemed them; and he bare them, and carried them all the days of old. KJB. Isaiah 63 verse 8 if we Obey the Lord are God and all these blessings will be ours KJB. Deuteronomy 28 KJB verse 2 And all these blessings shall come on thee, and overtake thee, if thou shalt hearken unto the voice of the Lord thy God. verse 15 But it shall come to pass, if thou wilt not hearken unto the voice of the Lord thy God, to observe to do all his commandments and his stautes which I command thee this day; that all these curses shall come upon thee, and overtake thee. if we don't obey God And we be unfaithful we will run in all kind bad luck so we must obey God by fasting and praying and going to the Throne of grace Ye adulterers and adulteresses, know ye not that the friendship of the world is enmity with God? Whosoever therefore will be a friend of the world is the enemy of God. KJB. James 4 verse 4 do not fellowship with the world is if you do you will fall and may not get back up you will suffer the consequences but with God there is hope for you in your everyday life we must obey him and trust the will of the Lord. Jesus takes care of his people when they obey him. The Lord knoweth the days of the upright; and their inheritance shall be for ever. Psalm 37 verse 18 KJB Psalm 37 KJB verse 3 Trust in the Lord, and do good; so shalt thou dwell in the land and verily thou shalt be fed. But seek ye first the kingdom of God and his righteousness; and all these things shall be added unto you KJB Matthew 6 verse 33 I have to think positive about life. I am very happy to be here this morning alive and well my God came through for me again he woke me up and start my day fresh, I think the lord for a another day thank you Jesus I acknowledged your name with a hard of thanksgiving I thankful for a new hope and your grace for the day I thank you O Lord for a great day, help me to have patient and have a peace in the Love of Christ in me and my family as well, help us not to give up in throw in the towel. I know we will still win the victory because we got you Jesus on are side I am glad you chose us to be your servants we not perfect but we serve a perfect God. KJB Psalm 41 verse 12 And as for me, thou upholdest me in mine integrity, and settest me before thy face forever. Verse 13 Blessed be the Lord God of Israel from everlasting, and to everlasting. A-men /, and Amen/, For with God nothing shall be impossible. Luke 1 verse 37 KJB. This I recall to my mind. Therefore have I hoped. It is of the Lord's mercies that we are not consumed, because his compassions fail not. They are new every morning great is thy faithfulness. The Lord is my portion saith my soul; therefore will I hope in him. The Lord is good unto them that wait for him, to the soul that seeketh him. The Lord is good unto them that wait for him, to the soul that seeketh him. It is good that a man should both hope and quietly wait for the salvation of the Lord. KJB Lamentations 3 verse23-24-25 verse 26 verse 31 For the Lord will not cast off for ever; verse 32-33 But though he cause grief, yet will he have compassion according to the multitude of his mercies, For he doth not afflict willingly nor grieve the children of men. Lamentations 3 KJB verse 40 Let us search and try our ways, and turn again to the Lord. Verse 41 let us lift up our heart with our hands unto God in the heavens. verse 55 I called upon thy name, O Lord, out of the low dungeon. Thou hast heard my voice; hide not thine ear at my breathing, at my cry. verse 57 Thou drewest near in the day that I called upon thee. Thou sadist, fear not. called you told me do not fear verse 58 O Lord thou hast pleaded the causes of my soul; thou hast redeemed my life. My Lord will save me from my enemies when they hurt me For they shall soon be cut down like the grass, and wither as the green herb. Psalm 37 verse2 KJB Luke KJB 6 verse 35 But love ye your enemies, and do good, and lend, hoping for nothing again; and your reward shall be great, and ye shall be the children of the highest; for he is kind unto the unthankful and to the evil. we sure focus on eternal life not the things of the world having your mine on jesus is the number one thing to do pay attention to God no your problems take it to the Lord in prayer keep your mine on Christ by reading the word of God or sharing Jesue with other unbelievers who need or want are help some will not receive what you say about God word here what God says in the bible And whosoever shall not receive you, nor hear your words, when ye depart out of that house or city, shake off the dust of your feet. KJB Matthew 10 verse 14 And Je'-sus came and spake unto them, saying All power is given unto me in heaven and in earth. Go ye therefore, and teach all nations, baptizing them in the name of the Father, and of the son, and of the Holy Ghost; Teaching them to observe all things, whatsoever I have commanded you; and I am with you always, even unto the end of the world A-men. Matthew KJB 28 verse 18-19-20 Follow me. John 21 vers 19 KJB No man can serve two masters; for either he will hate the one, and love other, Ye cannot serve God and mam-mon Matthew KJB 6 verse 24.

Be ye not unequally yoked together with unbelievers; for what fellowship hath righteousness with unrighteousness? And what communion hath light with darkness? And what concord hath Christ with Be'-lial? or what part hath he that believe with an infidel? 2 Corinthians 6 verse 14-16 KJB When the Spirt of truth comes, he will not speak on his own but will tell you what he has heard, he will tell you about the future KJB John 16-13 Howbeit when he, the spirt of truth, is come, he will guide you into all truth; for he shall not speak of himself; but whatsoever he shall, he speak; and he will shew you things to come. 1 John KJB verse 15-16 Love not the world, neither the things that are in the world. If any man love the world, the love of the Father is not in him. For all that is in the world, the lust of the flesh, and the lust of the eyes, and the pride of life, is not of the Father. But is of the world, verse 17 And the world passeth away, and the lust thereof; but he that doeth the will of God abideth for ever. Proverbs 15 verse 33 KJB The fear of the Lord is the instruction of wisdom; and before honour is humility. Proverbs 19 KJB verse verse 23 The fear of the Lord tendeth to life; and he that hatn it shall abide satisfied; he shall not be visited with evil. KJB Proverbs 10 verse 27 The fear of the Lord prolongeth days; but the years of the wicked shall be shortened. KJB Psalm 34 verse 8-9 O taste and see that the Lord is good; blessed is the man that trusteth in him. O fear the Lord, ye his saints; for there is no want to them that fear him. Verse 10 The young lions do lack, and suffer hunger; but they that seek the Lord shall not want any good thing. 1 Peter 2 verse 3 KJB if so be ye have tasted that the Lord is gracious. To whom coming, as unto a living stone, disallowed indeed of men, but chosen of God. And precious, Hebrew 10 verse 19 KJB Having therefore, brethren, boldness to enter into the holinest by the blood of Jesus, verse 20 By a new and living way. Which he hath consecrated for us, through the veil, that is to say, his flesh; verse 21 and having an high priest over the house of God; verse 22 Let us draw near with a true heart in full assurance of faith, having our hearts sprinkled from an evil conscience. And our bodlies washed with pure water. Verse 23 Let us hold fast the profession of our faith without wavering (for he is faithful that promised;) 1Corinthians 1 verse 9 KJB God is faithful, by whom ye were called unto the fellowship of his son Jesus Christ our Lord.

Romans KJB 10 verse 10 For with the heart man believeth unto righteousness; and with the mouth confession is made unto salvation. today Salvation by God reached me threw Grace because I obey Jesue when I going threw all kind of storms my God make away for me by speaking to me from the word of God he keeps me going in my everyday Circumstances But Still I Trust God in my trouble my example being connect to a Relationship with God means give my all to him I don't always worship like I should but I will try to go back to my daily visited to reached the throne of grace He answered and said unto them. Because it is given unto you to know the mysteries of the kingdom of heaven, but to them it is not given. For whosoever hath, to him shall be given, and he shall have more abundanc but whosoever hath not, from him shall be taken away even that he hath. Therefore speak I to them in parables; because they seeing see not; and hearing they hear not, neither do they understand. But he that received the seed into stony places, the same is he that heareth the word, and anon with joy receiveth it; Yet hath he not root in him-self, but dureth for a while; for when tribulation or persecution ariseth because of the word, by and by he is offended. He also that received seed among the thorns is he that heareth the word; and the care of this world. and the deceitfulness of riches, choke the word, and he becometh unfruitful. But he that received seed into the good ground is he that heareth the word, and understandeth it; which also beareth fruit, and bringeth forth, some an hundredfold, some sixty, some thirty. Matthew KJB 13 verse 11 12-13-14 threw20-21-22-23 Remember this my dear friends everyone must be quick to here but before you answer listen with a slow repond and not to get angry to fast. when you do what the word of God said in his way you never go wrong. Hebrews 2 KJB verse1 Therefore we ought to give the more earnest heed to the things which we have heard, lest at any time we should let them slip. But be ye doers of the word, and not hearers only deceiving your own selves. James 1 verse 22 KJB Are you listen to people he is speaking to you obey him is Rest in the Lord, and wait patiently for him; fret not thyself because of him who prospereth in his way, because of the man who bringeth wicked devices to pass; cease from anger; and forsake wrath fret not thyself in any wise to do evil. For evildoers shall be cut off; but those that wait upon the Lord, they shall inherit the earth; Psalm 37 verse7-8-9 KJB what he saying to you must walk close to Jesue in your prayer life. So you should maintain hope. from God he the only key to help in your everyday trials Important to allways walk with God at all times listen Jesue will respond oh Lord help me to pay attention and worshipt Matthew 6 verse 33 KJB. But seek ye frist the kingdom of God and his righteousness, and all these things shall be added unto you. Hebrews 13 KJB verse 5 Let your conversation be without covetousness; and be content with such things as ye have; for he hath said, I will never leave thee nor forsake thee. Believe in the possible. KJB. Philippian 1 KJB verse 4 Always in every prayer of mine for you all making request with joy, verse 5 for your fellowship in the gospel from the first day until now, verse 6 being confident of this very thing, that he which hatch begun a good work in you will perform it until the day of Jesue Christ, is by stating now to have fellowship with God ask Jesue in life right now he take you as you are repent. Ask God in your life and ask him to save you for Jesus sake and asks the Lord what to do. Regardless what going on in your life ether you have a bad day or good days even you don't understand obey and trust Jesue in your jouney everyday life. Mark 10 KJB. 27 And Jesus looking upon them saith, with men it is impossible, but not with God ; for with God all things are possible. Verse KJB Psalm 46 verse 10 Be still, and know that I am God. I will be honored by every nation I will be honored throng out the world. Wait on God. To take care of the circumstances Progress has all been providing with out delay God have you cover you. Your bless by the best. Genesis 18 verse 14 KJB anything too hard for the Lord. Proverbs KJB 8 verse 34 Blessed is the man that heareth me, watching daily at my gates, waiting at the posts of my doors. Verse 35 for whoso findeth me findeth life and shall otain favour of the

Lord. But he that sinneth against me wrongeth his own soul; all they that hate me love death KJB. John 12 verse 46 I am come a light unto the world, that whosoever believeth on me should not abide in darkness. verse 47 And if any man hear my words, and belive not, I judge him not; for I came not to judge the world, but to save the world, verse 48 He that rejecteth me, and receiveth not my words, hath one that judgeth him; the word that I have spoken, the same shall judge him in the last day. Verse 49 For I have not spoken of myself; but the Father which sent me, he gave me a commandment, what I should say, and what I should speak. My journey for the day God is precious to me he will be always my frist love in my life Psalms KJB. 36 verse 7 How excellent is thy lovingkindness, O God! Therefore the children of men put their trust under the shadow of thy wings. Verse 8 They shall be abundantly satisfied with the fatness of thy house; and thou shalt make them drink of the river of thy pleasures. CHAPTER 31 Today was A great day everything did work out according to God's plan I had my good days and my bad days But God Response to my prayer every chance he get when I call on God he answer Psalm 91 KJB verse 15 He shall call upon me, and I will answer him; I will be with him in trouble; I will deliver him and honour him. 2 Corinthians 12 KJB. Verse8 And he said unto me, My grace is sufficient for thee; for my strength is made perfect in weakness. KJB John 5 verse39 Search the scriptures; for in them ye think ye have eternal life; and they are they which testify of me. For God so love the world; that he gave his only begotten Son, that whosoever believeth in him should not perish, but have everlasting life. John 3 verse 16 KJB. I was going threw all kind of troubles but God had me cover by his grace he Established it before the founddation of the world, my emenies try to put all kind of interruptian like trying to trap me But God show up for me every time, Isaiah 41 verse 10 KJB. Fear thou not; for I am with thee; be not dismayed; for I am thy God; I will strengthen thee; yea; I will help thee yea, I will uphold thee with the right hand of my righteousness. My Lord will will keep me safe from all danger and he will keep my foot from falling in a trap he is my refuge, at all times I will put my trust in him. My God will help me when some one gives me trouble Jesue will be there on the double. And when I sick he is able to hill me.

This Lady my mom friend She was so funny she and her huband name was miss Bobbie Ann and mistard jakson they both was Laughable so funny in a nice kind of way miss bobie ann would shew her gum all day every day until the pont my brother OJ was nine at the time ask her do you sleep with your gum. One time my Mother and miss Bobbieann went rideing on a ornery day and my mom seen too big garbarg cans in the middle of the street and my mom drive around them and miss bobbie ann said Darnele why you going around for my mom said Bobbie Ann did you see that too big garbarg cans in the street No I did even see those garbarg cans I would had too cans, rideing under my car and my mom laugh so hard and tole are family about, and the other time she fell in the hall closet over my family house wen my dad was there at the time when Bill was over there for a visit that day see we had a walk in closet Bobbieann were talking and for she no It she fell right in the closet I thought was funny to my self MY dad was try ing not to laught so was daddy friend Bill came to visit too. Mister jakson pick her up ASK Her if she ok and all of us were consurn about her wellbeing but deep down in side we was had lots laughder to miss Bobbie ann was not hurt at all Thank God for that, that's was 1984 back in the days was fun times when my cosen toni was rideing with us and we went over the miss Bobbieann house my mom tole her don't stear at her she real funny she very laughable she will make you crack up Miss Bobbie Ann chewing her gum and talking very funny Toni was looking real close she was almost in her lap looking at her face with lagher. My mom said I tole you she is very funny to be around, This is a very funny story Once upon time miss bobbie ann was seting home watching television at night while her hursband was at work she hurt someone at her door she thought its was her son James she said James is that you she open the door all of a sudden she finely knew that was not her son James she look down the man did not have no pants on or shirt ether he just had a jacket on in flash her and Bobbie ann slam the door and lock it and shout out loud and and she made called to mistard Jakson her husband she said Jakson A naket man was at the door he said don't call me Bobbieann called the police, she love my mother cooking she was pitcing off the lemon cake my mom made for Bobbie Ann when we was over her house mistard Jackson was on the telephones he tole her write down the telephone number and Bobbie Ann was not even listening he look up and said you would not even listing what I was saying I tole you get peace paper and write down a phone number you busy piching off that cake Darnele made you those was the good old days as I sit back and look at my cat gemi he remind me of old cat gemi the frist he was a very smart cat too smart for his good he would get In lots of troble one time we brought him so cat food he did like it he would cover it up with his other food pan lets us no he would eat it some time my brother would go by him some cat food because the cat would starve his self he would eat a hole day unless you by the cat food he like sometimes the cat would bring a chipmont from outside and run threw the house with the chip month in his mouth we had to close all the doors in the house so he would not get in are rooms MY Granmom was there to visit and she was there when the cat had chase the chip month all over the house Granmom got scard and jump on the top of the chair and finey my brother Paul hit the chip moth with the broon and everything was over the cat stop chacing the chip moth and the chip month was no more, and others times are cat gemi would boss my daddy my mother would telll gemi way until granddaddy come home she says to the cat the cat would get in front of the door and wait for my dad come home and when he came home my dad would sit down and read the news paper and he would say gemi the cat gemi would you doing gemmie the cat would look at the door and start shouting out loud let him no he won't go out side some time my daddy would not listen and go back to the news paper and the cat would jump up and grabb the news paper out my father hand and throw the news paper on the flood and pull his paw over it and look at him and he let him no he meen bussnes. One thanksgiving the cat got in the turkey he loves turkey see the cat would get a table scaps of turkey from all of us he from me OJ. larmont mom and dad the cat walk in the room and flap his self down in the bed he slept for the whole day until turkey time again. one time he wait until all of us went to sleep and the cat gemi has Is way on the top of the stove of and he got in the pot and took the cover off the pot and took that whole turkey out and got on the floor and had a feast on the turkey the next moring mom got up and saw the cat on the floor with are turkey she was not pleace with that cat my mom whip that cat and put him out side for hole day. That's the thanksgiving we never forgot, I Remamber one time this man my father try to sposer A man from AA his name is Gene he was drugs bad and his mom put him out her house he had no place to stay and my dad wanted Gene stay at are house on the sofa that night my mom did not won't mister Gene in are house my mom had put her too sense and and are cat spoke something too in cat talk shouting to my dad too we were surprise the cat spoke his words My mom said even gemi the cat did not want him ther e ether So my mom put him out and mistard Gene had to sleep in the car I what not blame my mom mistard Gene were on drugs, my dad was only try to help but I say my mom did the right thang, But God hath chosen the foolish things of the world to confound the wise;and God hath chosen the weak things which are mighty' 1Coninthians 1 KJB verse 27 verse28 And base things of the world, and things which are despised, hath God chosen, yea, and things which are not, to bring to nought things that are; verse 29 That no flesh should glory in his presence. Verse 30 But of him are ye in Christ Jesus, who of God is made unto us wisdom, and righteousness, and sanctification and redemption; verse 31 That, according as it is written, he that glorieth, let him glory in the Lord. I had a good day I was going threw storms but God is still in control I still press him my week was ok by the grace of God he is allsume to me always he keeps his promies all of the time I went to my daddy house my family and I my baby brother birtday was toaday he turn 3 years old he from by father second wife we had a good time we had cake and Ice cream my brother had a Lots of presents we had a good whole time my family am I and a old friend from school we grown up with back In the days we all had a good time, The love of God is with you in grace and peace in a time of trouble and turmoil remember nothing can separate us from the love of God-this is peace in the midst of the storm, by a paster my Lord is always ready to be merciful to me and his people and he will have pity on us when we doing right when we trust in the Lord he always have conpassion on us. And therefore will the Lord wait that he may be gracious unto you, and therefore will he be exalted, that he may have mercy upon you; for the Lord is a God of judgment; blessed are all they that wait for him. For the people shall dwell in Zion at Jerusalem; thou shalt weep no more; he will be very gracious unto thee at the voice of thy cry; when he shall hear it, he will answer thee. KJB. Isaiah 30 verse 18-19 before talking about the word we need to read the guidance of God word and every day life. For this God is our God for ever and ever; he will be our guide ever unto death. KJB. Psalm 48 verse 14 Believe in God no matter how your breakthrew has not come yet but still have a positive attitude seen like you running all over the community try to find a job and the people slameing the doore on you for me myself and I been there and done that but still God is amble to help me it is very painful when people hurt you having you believe they will help you but they just playing you along like they for you but really deep down they don't care if you make it or not with Jesue on my side I will make It and I look toward to a brighter future I will take of you Jeremiah, Jeremiah KJB. 15 verse 11 The Lord said, Verily it shall be well with thy remnant; Exodus 33 KJB. Verse 14 And he said, My presence shall go with thee, and I will give thee rest. KJB. 2 Corinthians 6verse For he saith, I have heard thee in a time accepted. And in the day of salvation have I succoured thee; behold, now is the accepted time; behold, now is the day of salvation), when you believe in God is on your side he make things you hope for will sudden change, when people treat you like garbarg God turn it out for his good tressure, but one day my God will make me and his chosen people famons. My God will help those who have fallen. And he will carry them and lifts them up and he will bent over backwards for his children and bent beneath their loads. When the wicked do me wrong my Lord will help me. The eyes of all look to you In hope Philipians 4 KJB verse 13 For I can do all things through Christ which strengtheneth me. even So you have done well to share with in my present difficuhy.

One day I enter a contest but its was all set up these people were not right at all they protent they were for me but they were all agaist me they try to shame so I could trop out of the contest but God is in control he is able to work it out and he did show up and everthing work out according to his plan. God reminds us I heard my call in the nick of time God knows I need him he always help me when I need. He will always there when I need help you need me I was there to help, KJB. 1John 5 verse 14 And this is the confidence that we have in, him that, if we ask any thing according to his will he heareth us; verse 15 And if we know that he hear us, whatsoever we ask, we know that we have the petition that we desired of him. KJB. But it is good for me to draw near to God; that I may declare all thy works. Psalm 73 verse 28 well I past with flying colors my enemies was the one were put to shame and the people like my act That's was But God help me and I stole the show By God GRAZE I made it. Psalm KJB. 94 verse 18 When I said, My foot slippeth; thy mercy, O Lord, help me up. For David speaketh concerning him, I forsaw the Lord always before my face, for he is on my right hand, that I should not be moved; Therefore did my heart rejoice, and my tongue was glad; more over also my flesh shall rest in hope; KJB. Act 2-25-26, My Lord will not abandon me or leave me as orphans in the storm. Take the word of God and read it for your self and see and pray and believe his promise for your life. O taste and see that the Lord is good; blessed is the man that trusteth in him O fear the Lord, ye his saints; for there is no want to them that fear him. KJB. Psalm 34 verse 8-9 And he said, My presence shall go with thee, and I will give thee rest. Exodus KJB. 33 verse KJB. 14. John 14 verse 1 Let not your heart be trouble; ye believe in God, believe also in me. When you have a Relationship God with you never go wrong and regardless what going on in your circumstances God have you cover by his grace there is hope in my future by God stardard he will make me great. The Lord said, Verily it shall be well with thy remnant; KJB by doing God's will are future look very good by hopeing in the Lord. Put your trust in God not yourself or others but the Lord. Know body can help us but Jesue but wait and see how he is good. The Lord will not leave him when he is judge Wait on the Lord, and keep his way, and he shall exalt thee to inherit the land; when the wicked are cut off, thou shalt see it. KJB. Psalm 37 verse 33-KJB. Romams 8 verse 25 But if we hope for that we see not, then do we with patience wait for it. verse 26 Likewise the Spirit also helpeth our infirmities for we know not ought; but the Spirit itself maketh intercession for the saints according to the will of God. KJB. James 1 verse 4-5 But let patience have her perfect work, that ye may have her perfect and entire, wanting nothing. If any of you lack wisdom, let him ask of God, that giveth to all men liberally, and upbraideth not; and it shall be given him.

Entertainment of this world is not important we must focus on Jesue not the evil thangs but the unturnal things Love not the world, neither the things that are world neither the things that are in the world. If any man love the world. The love of the Father is not in him. For all that is in the world, the lust of the flesh, and the lust of the eyes, and the pride of life, is not of the Father but of the world. KJB. 1John 2 verse 15 verse 16-17 And the world passeth away, and the lust thereof; but he that doeth the will of God abideth for ever. Verse 18 Little children, it is the last time; and as ye have heard that an(-ti-christ shall come, even now are ther many a(ti-christs; whereby we know that it is the last time. Verse 19 They went out from us, but they were not of us; for if they had been of us, they would no doubt have continued with us; but they went out, that they might be made manifest that they were not all of us. Verse 20 But ye have an unction from the Holy One, and ye know all things. Verse 21 so I have not written unto you because ye know not the truth, but because ye know it, and that no lie is of the truth. Verse 22 Who is a liar but he that de-nieth that Jesus is the Christ? He is an(-ti-christ, that denieth the Father and the son. Verse 23 Whosoever denieth the son, the same hath not the Father; (but) he that acknowledgeth the Son hath the father also. Verse 24 Let that therefore abide in you, which ye have heard from the beginning. If that which ye have heard from the beginning shall remain in you, ye also shall continue in the Son, and in the Father. Verse 25 And this the promise that he hath promised us, even eternal life. Verse 26 These things have I have I written unto you concerning them that seduce you. verse 27 But the anointing which ye have received of him abideth in you, and ye need not that any man teach you; but as the same anointing teacheth you of all things, and is truth, and is no lie, and even as it hath taught you, ye shall abide in him. Verse 28 And now, little children. Abide in him; that, when he shall appear, we may have confidence, and not be ashame before him at his coming. Verse29 If ye know that he is righteous, ye know that every one that deeth righteousness is born of him. the Lord, Jeremiah KJB. 39 verse 18 For I will surely deliver thee, and thou shalt not fall by the sword, but thy life shall be for a prey unto thee; because thou hast put thy trust in me, saith the Lord. Ah Lord God! Behold, thou hast made the heaven and the earth by thy great power and nothing too hard for thee; KJB. Jeremiah 32 verse 17 Thus said the Lord the king of Israel, and his redeemer the Lord of hosts; I am the frist, and I am the last; and beside me there is no God. KJB. Isaiah 44 verse 6-8 Son, thy sins be forgiven thee. KJB. Mark 2 verse 5 many are called but those are eleck my God are ready been chosen before the foundation of the world and that only but a few. Obey the Lord then it will go well with you. this is a new beginning for me for the day God is so good he took care of me I believe he grab of hole of me and huge me and let me no he love me he spoke the word from the bible, the good book said to me Favour is deceitful and beauty is vain; but a woman that feareth the Lord, she shall be praised. Give her of the fruit of her hands; and let her own works praise her the gates. KJB. Proverbs 31 verse 30 It is good for me that I have been afflicted; that I might learn thy statutes. verse 71 The law of thy mouth is better unto me than thousands of gold and silver. Psalm 119 verse 72 KJB. Verse 73-80 Thy hands have made me and fashioned me; understanding that I may learn thy commandments. Thou puttest away all the wicked of the earth like dross; therefore I love thy testimonies. Psalms 119-129-136 KJB. Thy testimonies are wonderful; therefore doth my soul keep them. Verse135 Make thy face to shine upon thy servant; and teach me thy statues. Rivers of waters run down mine eyes, because they keep not thy law. A call to live holy. Wherefore grid up the loins of your mind, be sober, and hope to the end for the grace that is to be brought unto you at the revelation of Jesus Christ; KJB. 1 Peter 1 verse13 VERSE 14 As obedient children, not fashioning yourselves according to the former lust in your ignorance; verse 15 But as he which hath called you is holy, so be ye holy in all manner of conversation; verse 16 Because it is written, Be ye holy; for Iam holy. Verse 17And if ye call on the Father, who without respect of persons judgeth according to every man's work. Pass the time of your so-jouring here in fear verse 18 Forasmuch as ye know that ye were not redeemed with corruptible things, as silver and gold, from your vain conversation received by tradtion from your fathers; verse 19 But with the precious blood of Christ, as of a lamb without blemish and without spot; verse 20 Who verity was foreordained before the foundation of the world, but was manifest in these last times for you, verse 21 Who by him do believe in God, that raised him up from the dead, and gave him glory; that your faith and hope might be in God verse 22 Seeing ye have purified your souls in obeying the truth throught the Spirit unto unfeigned love of the brethren, see that ye love one another with a pure heart fervently;Being born again, not of corruptible seed, but of incorruptible, by the word of God, which liveth and abideth for ever. Verse 23 word word of God verse 24 For all flesh is as grass, and all the glory of man as the flower of grass, the grass withereth, and the flower thereof falleth away; But the word of the Lord endureth for ever. And this theword which by the gospel is preached unto you. Because I trusted in the Lord he will give my reward for the rest of my life. According to his word he has spoken it, And with his hand he will resue me from harm. Matthew 9 KJB. Verse 28 Believe ye that I am able to do this? Obeying is better than saying I'm sorry.

1 Samuel KJB. 15 verse 22 And Samuel said, Hath the Lord as great delight in burnt offerings and sacrifices, as in obeying the voice of the Lord? Behole, to obey is better than sacrifice, and to hearken than the fat of rams. We have to continue to obey God word and his will I regret would I did in my past I go to God and repent of my sens when do wrong, to my family and to others people I ask God to forgive me on my everyday life Because we not perfect but we serve a perfect God. Rebellion is as sinful as witch craft, and stubbornness as bad as worhiping idols, so because you have rejected the command of the Lord he has rejected you asking, So do the right thing and give to the Lord in prayer and obey his will Seek the Lord in prayer and repent of your sens he will save us with his grace for the Lord God is a sun and shield the Lord will give grace and glory no good thing will he with hold from them that walk uprightly. KJB. Psalm 84 verse 11 But they that wait upon the Lord shall renew their strength they shall mount up with wings as eagles; they shall run and not be weary. And they shall walk and not faitnt KJB. Isaiah 40 verse 31 See my Lord known me and his people well and he said we are special. Deuteronomy 4 verse 29 KJB. But if from thence thou shalt seek the Lord thy God, thou shalt find him. If thou seek him with all thy heart and with all thy soul. Jeremiah 29 KJB verse 13 And ye shall seek me, and find me, when ye shall search for me with all your heart. KJB Psalms 36 verse 7 How excellent is thy lovingkindness, O God! Therefore the children of men put their trust under the shadow of thy wings. Set your affection on things above, not on things on earth. KJB. Colossians 3 verse 2 For whoso findeth me findeth life, and shall obtain favour of the Lord But he that sinneth against me wrongeth his own soul; all they that hate me love death. KJB. Proverbs 8 verse 35-36 KJB. Hear ye therefore the parable of the sower. When any one heareth the word

of the kingdom, and understandeth it not, then cometh the wicked one, and catcheth away that which was sown in his heart. This is he which received seed by the way side. But he that received the seed into stony places, the same is he that heareth the word, and anon with joy receiveth it; Yet hath he not root in himself; but dureth for a while; for when tribulation or persecution ariseth because of the word, by and by he is offended. KJB. Matthew 13 18-19-20-21-22-23-Hear ye therefore the parable of the sower. When any one heareth the word of the kingdom. And understand it not, then cometh the wicked one, and catcheth away that which was sown in his heart. This is he which received seed by the way side. But he that received the seed into stony places, the same is he that heareth the word, and anon with joy receiveth it; Yet hath he not root in himself, but dureth for a while; for when tribulation or persecution ariseth because of the word, by and by he is offended. He also that received seed amomg the thorns is he that hear among the thorns is he that heareth the word; and the care of this world, and the deceitfulness of riches, choke the word, and he become unfruitful. Vers 23 But he that received seed into the good ground is he that heareth the word, and understandeth it; which also beareth fruit, and bringeth forth, some an hundredfold, some sixty, some thirty. KJB. Psalm 33 verse 11 The counsel of the Lord standeth for ever, the thoughts of his heart to all generations. As a athlete we must run in a race by winning the prize and obeying the rules is the key to win.

KJB. 2 Timothy4 verse 8-9 Henceforth there is laid up for me a crown of righteousness, judge, Shall give me at that day; and not to me only, but unto all them also that love his appearing. Do thy diligence to come shortly unto me; KJB. PsalmKJB. 25 verse 4 Shew me thy ways, O Lord; teach me thy paths. KJB. Verse 5 Lead me in thy truth, and teach me; for thou art the God of my salvation; on thee do I wait all the day. Verse 6 Remember, O Lord, thy tender mercies and thy lovingkindnesses; for they have been ever of old. Verse 7 Remember not the sins of my youth, nor my transgressions; according to thy mercy remember thou me for thy goodness' sake, O Lord. Verse 8 Good and upright is the Lord; therefore will he teach sinners in the way. Verse 9 The meek will he guide in judgment; and the meek will he teach his way. Verse10 All the paths of the Lord are mercy and truth unto such as keep his covenant and his testimonies, All who put your hope in the Lord. Should never be put to shame. Blessed is he whose transgression is forgiven. Psalm 32 verse 1-2-3-4-5-6-7-8-9-10 Psalm 121 verse5-8 KJB The Lord is thy keeper; the Lord is thy shade upon thy right hand. The Lord shall preserve thy going out and thy coming in from this time forth, and even for ever more. I even I, am the Lord; and beside me there is no savior. I have declared, and have saved, and I have shewed, when there was no strange god among you; therefore ye are my witnesses, saith the Lord, that I am God. KJB Isaiah 43 verse 11-12 verse 13 Yea, before the day was I am he; and there is none that can deliver out of my hand;I will work, and who shall let it? Verse 19 Behold, I will do a new thing; now it shall spring forth; shall ye not know it? I will even make a way in the wilderness, and rivers in the desert. verse 21 This people have I formed for myself; they shall shew forth my praise, My Jouney for today was perfect my God show up by his grace I am save today Regardless what my circumstances I will

still praise God he help me and in the past and I no God will help me in my future as well the outcome will be good For by grace are ye saved through faith; and that not of yourselves; it is the gift of God; KJB. Ephesians 2 verse 8 we have to keep are mind on the Lord when we go thought trouble trust in God and also trust in Jesue because one day the Lord will prepare a place in heaven that will be are home some day where the Father lives one day when God ready for us he will take us up to the heavenly home and we will always live with the Lord forever. And Jesue is the only way to get there. Jesus saith unto him, I am the way, the truth. And the life; no man cometh unto the Father, but by me. John 14 Verse 6 KJB. But it is good for me to draw near to God; I have put my trust in the Lord God, that I may declare all thy works. KJB. Psalm 73 verse 28 Preserve me, O God; for in thee do I put my trust. Psalm 16 verse 1 Thou wilt shew me the path of life in thy presence is fulness of joy; at thy right hand there are pleasures for evermore, KJB. Psalms 16 verse 11.

And who shall also confirm you unto the end, that ye may be blameless in the day of our Lord Jesus Christ. KJB 1Corinthians 1 verse 8-9 God will always does just what he says, and he is the one who invited you into this wonderful friend ship with his son, even christ our Lord. For God hatch not given us the spirit of fear but of power and of a sound mind. KJB. 1Timothy 1 verse 7 All my Life I use fear of what may happen back then I did not belive in my self but God had my back every step off the way in my history he never fell me yet I am going threw storm but God is ample to bring me out and help me up when I fall. My Lord always has put all the pieces of the puzzle together in my everyday life he is endless with God I wiil achive my goals in my life. If you put your trust in the Lord will never be put to shame. If the wicked put you by Embarrassment from hold lots of people when you going threw difficulty God will put them in shame. And Ha'man answered the king, For the man whom the king delighteth to honour, verse 8 Let the royal apparel be brought which the king useth to wear, and the horse that the king rideth upon, and the crown royal which is set upon his head; verse 9 And let this apparel and horse be delivered to the hand of one of the king's most noble princes, that they may array the man withal whom the king delighteth to honour, and bring him on horseback through the street of the city, and proclaim before him, Thus shall it be done to the man whom the king delighteth to honour. Verse 10 Then the king said to Ha'-man, Make haste, and take the apparel and the horse as thou hast said, and the horse, as thou hast said, and do even so Mor'-de-cai the Jew, that sitteth at the king's gate; let nothing fail of all that thou hast spoken. Verse 11 Then took Ha'-man the apparel and the horse, and arrayed Mor'-de-cai, and brought him on horseback through the street of the city, and proclaimed before him. Thus shall it be done unto the man whom the king delight-eth to honour. Verse 12 And Mor'-de-cai came again to the king's gate. But Ha'-man hasted to house mourning, and having his head coverd.

KJB. ESTHER 6 7-8-9-10-11-12 Know ye not that the unrighteous shall not inherit the kingdom of God? Be not deceived; neither fornicators, nor idolaters, nor adulterers, nor effeminate, nor abusers of themselves with mankind, verse 10 Nor thieves, nor covetous, nor drunkards, nor revilers, nor extortioners, shall inherit the kingdom of God. Verse 11 And are washed, but ye are sanctified, but ye are justified in the name of the Lord Jesus, and by the Spirt of our God. KJB. 1 Corinthians 6 verse 9-10-11 Flee fornication. Every sin that a man doeth is without the body; but he that committeth fornication sinneth against his own body. verse 18 Thou shalt not lie with mankind, as with womankind; it is abomination. KJB. Leviticus 18 verse 22 lest thou give thine honour unto others. And thy years unto the cruel; lest strangers be filled with thy wealth; and thy labours be in the house of a stranger; And thou mourn at the last, when thy flesh and thy body are consumed. KJB. Proverbs 4 verse 5-9-11 Her feet go down to death; her steps take hold on hell. I no these people I ministry too about homosexual some thank me for telling them and other respond was not nice about it I got yell at in this company I use to work for back in the days not to bring the word of God on my Job no more even when I not on the clock, now some of the people who did me wrong at the time got fired at the time one person got fired for stealing from the gas stion one was taking to ER and and also got fired as well and other person got real ill I did not no who that person was as that person was as black as cole and aids consumes that person body took his tole, As the whirlwind passeth, so is the wicked no more; but the righteous is an everlasting foundation. KJB. Proverbs 10 verse 25 Treasures of wickedness profit nothing; but righteousness delivereth from death. KJB. Proverbs 10 verse 2 when I going threw struggles and depression I have a close walk with God each day of the time praying and daily devotion keeps me going I look back on my memories what he brought me throught in my past and say why do I worried or get sad God is able to work it out on my behave on every day life. I think positive even my plan don't work out at the time is always is a brighter tomorrow that's my testimony trust Jesue and watch what happen keep on believing what you hope for when you got God he will fight your battles he willl show up on time He mite not come when he want to but will always show up on time. That the trial of your faith, being much more precious than of gold that perisheth though it be tried with fire, might be found unto praise and honour and glory at the appearing of Jesus Christ; KJB. 1 Peter T I Peter 1 verse 8-9 and 13-16 a life energetic and blazing with holiness God said I am holy you be holy. Verse 17 you call out to God for helps-he's a good father that way. But don't forget he's also a responsible father and won't let you get by with sloppy living. Verse 18-21 your life is a journey you must travel with a deep consciousness of God. It cost God plenty to get you out of that dead end empty-headed life you grew up in. whoever rejects this teaching is rejecting a human being, but God who gives you his his holy spirit 1Thessalonians 4 verse 8 God wants you be holy and completely free from sexual immorality. Each of you should know how to live with your wife in holy and honorable pay, each of you should know how to live with your wife in holy and honorable pay not with a Lustful desire, like the heather who do not know God. In this matter then none of you should do wrong to other Christians or take advantage of them. We have told you this before, and we strongly warned you that the Lord will punish those who do that God did not call us to live in immorality but in holiness so then 1Thessalonign 4 verse 4-5-6-7 whoever rejects this teaching is rejecting a human being, but God who gives you his holy spirit. Make it your aim to live a quiet life. To mind your own bussiness. And to earn your own living just as we told you before in this way you will win the respect of those in this way you will win the respect of those who are not believers. And you will not have to depend on anyone for what you need, 1 Thessalonians 4 verse 8-11-12 Dear Jesue I am trying Everyday of my life try to walk like Christ like. Please help me to obey you in every step of the way, here my acoriding to my records I had a nerves break down I was kick use hurt abandon Laugh at spite in the face and all most fell in my life But God you were with me every step of the way but I am still alive by God grace I am still alive today Who has believed our message To whom has the Lord revealed his powerful arm. My servant grew up in the Lord's presence like tender green shoot, like a root in dry ground. There was nothing beautiful or majestic about his appearance. Nothing to attract us to him He was depised and rejected a man of sorrows acquainted with deepest grief. We turned our backs on him and looked the other way. He was our weaknesses he carried; it was our sorrows that weighed him down. And we thought his troubles were a punishment from God, a punishment for his own sins But he was pierced for our rebellion. Crushed for our sins. He was beaten so we could be whole. He was whipped so we could be healed. All of us, like sheep, have strayed away. We have left God's paths to follow our own. Yet the Lord laid on him the sins of us all. He was oppressed and treated harshly, yet he never said a word. He was led like a lamb to the slaughter. And as a sheep is silent before the shearers, he did not open his mouth. Unjustly condemned, he was led away. No one cared that he died without descendants that his life was cut short in midstream but he was struck down for the rebellion of my people. He had done no wrong and had never deceived anyone. But he was buried like a criminal he was put in a rich man's grave. But it was the Lord's good plan to crush him and cause him grief Yet when his life is made an offering for sin, he will have many descendants. He will enjoy a long life, and the Lord's good plan will prosper in his hands. When he sees all that is accomplished by his anguish, he will be satisfied. And because of his experience, my righteous servant will make it possible for many to be counted righteous. For he will bear all their sins. I will give him the honors of a victorious soldier. Because he exposed himself to death. He was counted among the rebels. He bore the sins of many and interceded for rebels, ISAIAH 53 VERSE 1-12 Page 129 that's the word of God, and he also says Come my Children and listen to me, and I will teach you to fear the Lord, does anyone want to live a life that is long and prosperous. Then keep your tongue from speaking evil and your lips from telling lies turn away from evil and do good search for peace and work to maintain it. The eyes of the Lord watch over those who his ears are open to cries for help but the Lord turns his face against those who do evil. He will erase their memory from the earth. The lord hears his people when they call him for help He rescues them from all their troubles the lord come to the resue each time. For the lord protects. The bones of the righteous. Not one of them is broken calamity will surely overtake the wicked and those who hate the righteous will be punised, but the Lord will redeem those who serve him, No one who who takes refuge in him will be condemned Psalm 34 11-27 For I am about to do something new, see, I have already begun do you not see it Isaiah 44 verse 19 Don't let your heart be troubled. Trust in God and trust also in me, there is more than enough room in my Father's home. If this were not so would I have told you that I am going to prepare a place for you. When everything is ready I will come and get you. So that you will always be with me where I am and you know the way to where I am going, No we don't know Lord, Thomas said we have no idea where you are going so how can we know the way Jesus told him I am the way the truth and the life, no one can come to the father except through me. John 14 verse 1-6 I have followed all his regulations I have never abandoned his decrees. I am blameless before God I have kept myself from sin the Lord reared me for doing right. He has seen my innocence, 2 Sanuel 22 verse 23 Remember this good deed also, o my God, have compassion on me according to your great and unfailing love Nehemiah 13 verse 22 This what the Lord says for I know the plans I have for you says the Lord, they are plans for good not for disaster to give you a future and hope, in those days when you pray I Will listen if you look for me wholeheartedly you will find me. I will be found by you says thew Lord Jeremiah 29 verse 11 Graduation you beem promoted Love Jesue the Lord and your saver. Listen says Jesue, I am coming soon I will bring my reward with me to give to each one according to what he has done I am the frist and the last the beginning and the end Revelation 22 verse 12 Happy are those who wash their robes clean and so eat the fruit from the tree of life and to go through the gates unto the city, verse 14 Once you received no mercy; now recived God's mercy. 1Peter 2 verse 10 Page 130 verse 11 Dear friends I warm you as temporary resdents and foreigners" to keep away from worldly desires that wage war against your very souls. Verse 12 Be careful to live properly among your unbelieving neighbors. Then even if they accuse you of doing wrong, they will give honor to God when he judges the world yet we who have this spiritual treasure are like common clay pots, in order to show that the supreme power belongs to God not to us 2 Corinthians 4 verse 7 I have the strength to face all conditions by the power that Christ gives me. Philippians 4 verse 13 in conclusion, my friends, fill your minds with those things that are good and that desrve praise things that are true, noble right pure lovely and honorable. Put unto practice what you learned and received from me both from my words and from my actions. And God who gives us peace will be with you. Philpians 4 verse 8 Don't worry about anything but in all your prayers asking him with a thankful heart. Verse 7 and God's peace, which is far beyond human understanding, will keep you hearts and minds safe in union with Christ Jesus, Philippians 4 verse 6 I am determined to to do the will of God No matter what come my way God have everything undercontrol he will bless me in his time no matter who reject you God says he will adcerpt. you I determined not to give up on God because he not give up on me, This is the Lord's doing it is marvelous in our eyes, Psalm 118 verse 23 I try to keep my mine focused on Christ Jesue committed to God is my life line my goats will take progress keeping and watching and waiting and praying and looking toward God is the answer. He will never abandon me or throw me away, obstacle may come But God will pursuid my goals on the right time and use people to bless me in the right place, you got to wait for your time, But when you pray go into your room close the door and pray to your Father who is unseen. Then your Father who sees what is done in secret will reward you, Matthes 5 verse 6 we have to believe in Christ Jesue who can do what he said he can do For a person who doesn't believe in Christ, God son can't have God the Father either. But he who has Christ God's son has God the Father also So keep on believing what you have been taught from the beginning, if you do you will always be in close fellowship with both God the Father and his son And he himself has promised us this external life, These remarks of mine about the antichrist are pointed at those who would dearly love to blind fold you and lead you astray. But you have received the holy spirit and he lives within you in your hearts, so that you don't need anyone to teach you what is right, for he teaches you all things and he is the truth, and no liar; and so just as he has said you must live in Christ never to depart from him, And now my little children, stay in happy fellowship with the Lord so that when he comes you will be sure that all is well and will not have not have to be ashamed and shrink back from meeting him Since we know that God is always good and does only right we may rightly assume that all those who do right are his children, Stop loving this evil world and all that it offers you, for when you love these things you show that you do not really love God for all these worldy things, these evil desires the craze for sex the ambition to buy everything that appeals to you and the pride that comes from wealth and importance-these are not from God they are from this evil world itself and this world is fading away and these evil forbidden things will go with it, but whoever keeps doing the will of God will live forever. Dear children, this world's last hour has come you have heard about the antichrist who is commming the one who is against Christ and already many such person have appeared, the makes us all the more certain that the end of the world is near. These against Christ people used to be members of our churches but they never really belonged with us or else they would have stayed. When they left us it proved that they were not of us at all But you are not like that for the holy spirit has come upon you and you know the truth So I am not writing to you as to those who need to know the truth but I warn you as those who can discern the difference between true and false and who is the greatest liar the one who says that Jesus is not Christ such a person is antichrist for he does not believe in God the Father and in his son. For a person who doesn't believe in Christ, God's son can't have God the father either but he who has Christ God's son has God the father also. Page 131 For this God is our God forever and ever he will be our guide even unto dearth. Psalm 48 verse 14 God is our refuge and strength a very present help in trouble. Psalm 46 verse 1 Give your burdens to the Lord. And he will take care of you he will not permit the godly to slip and fall, but you o God will send the wicked down to the pit destruction murderers and lious will die young But I am truting you to save me, Psalm 55 verse 23 O God have mercy on me my foes attack me all day long They are always twisting what I say they spend their days plotting to harm me. They come together to spy on me watching my every step eager to kill me, don't let them get away with their wickedness in your anger o god bring them down you keep thack of all my sorrows. You have collected all my tears in your bottle you have recorded each one in your book my enemies will retreat when I call to you for help this I know God is on my side, I praise God for what he has promised yes, I praise the Lord for what has promised. I trust in God so why should I be afraid what can mere mortals do to me Psalm 56 verse 1-2-3-4-5-6-8-9-10-11 We are ambassadors for christ since God is making his appeal through us 2 Corinthians 5 verse16-21 Since you have been raised to new life with christ set your sight on the realities of heaven Colossians 3 verse3 Jesue said I am the light of the world. Whoever follow me will never walk in darkness but will have the light of life. John 8 verse 8 Let all the world look to me for salvation for I am God there is no other I have sworn by my own name I have spoken the truth and I will never go back on my word; everyknee will bend to me and every tongue will confess allegiance to me the people will declare the Lord is the source of all my righteousness and strength and all who were angry with him will come to him and be ashamed in the Lord all the generations of Israel will be justified and in him they will boast. Isaiah 45 verse 22-23-24-25 The name of the Lord is a strong fortress the godly run to him and are safe. Proverbs 18 verse 10 Rejoice in our confident hope be patient in trouble and keep on praying. When God's people are in need be ready to help them always be eager to practice hospitality Romans 12 verse 15 Are any among you sick they should call for the elders of the church and have them pray over them anointing them with oil in the name of Lord James 14 in one of the verse Walk in the way of the good and keep to the paths of the just for the upright will abide in the land and the innocent will remain in it Matthew 7 verse 13-14 Wait on the Lord be of good courage. And he shall strengthen thine art wait I say on the Lord. Psalm 27 verse 16 Know therefore that the lord thy God he is God the faithful God which keepth covenant and mercy with them that Love him and keep his commandments to a thousand generations Deuteronomy 7 verse 9 Trust in the Lord with all thine heart and learn not unto thine own understanding in all thy ways acknoledge him and he shall direct thy paths. Proverbs 3 verse 5-6 It is of the Lord's mercies that we are not consumed, because his compassions fail not. They are new every morning great is thy faihfulness. Lamentations 3 verse 22-23 Thy righteousness is like the great mountains thy judgments are a great deep o Lord thou preservest man and beast. Psalm 36 verse 6 The sun shall be no more thy light by day neither for brightness shall the moon give light unto thee but the Lord shall be unto thee anto thee an everlasting Light and thy God thy glory, Isaiah 60 verse 9 My weekening was very successful I had good time I went on vacation tript we went on chunch Convension with my other chunch we went out my self and sister peggie Fransise Mother rose Mother betty Paster Lee his wife Sister lucy And there little granson Littie Jon we had very good time we left about 1015 in the Moring we on the road as we were past by we a lots mountains tops all around its something I never seen before. So the woman and I had connect we talk and Laught all threw the day about 5 we made back to the hotel every body had rooom a pice the psaster and his wife and they had a room and the too mother of the church also had a room my self and I peggie Fransise we had a room also we went back to change for n at 7 the paster said be down stairs at 6 pm we all were down stairs n time. Sister lucy peach the word the service was alsume she pearch pray to young and old we had good time by God grace we had good time we were bless by the best that Jesue Christ the Lord. I will faithfully reward my people and make an eternal covenant with them, They will be famous among the nations, Everyone who sees them will know that they are a people whom I have blessed, Isaiah 61 verse 8-9 Page 132 we all us had good Fellowship all threw the day and after we eating from the restrant we all went back to the holtel and all us went to sleep I got up at 8am shower and dress and sister peggie and sister fransise went to eat breakfast downstaris and myself we had pancakes fruit and oatmeal and OJ AND Fransise had coffee and after breakfaust we all went back up to are room. They went back to sleep as for me I stay up and watch television and trying to my devoisiom at the same time and I forgot my jounal so I ask sister Peggie was a gife shop down stairs she said it mite be so I went down to the hotel Lobbie to find out So I acts one of the worker at the hotel she said one the store is cross of street so went back to the room upstairs and got lost I did I no what floor what I was on But I for got the room number here

I am knoking on the door saying sister peggie are in this room and paster Lee answer the door I said brother Lee I got lose he oh on and he tole his wife sister lucy called sister peggie come to the door Renee got lost then sister Yolanda one of the member chuch show were to go and sister peggie open the door and fransise were saying who is that she was sleeping and herd us she wonder was going on after I told then what happen we all had big laught about and I thought was kind of funny, it all work out according to his plan because I was not afraid Because I trust God. DO not be afraid Matthew 10 verse 28 Page 133 Psalm 16 in one of the chapter I will bless the Lord who guides me even at night my heart instruds me. Your callaufive for a blessing and your enemy no this and he watching you because he is in fear he no God has your back so he is trying to his best to break you. But God stept in every time, When you have God on your side you can't not lose. No weapon that is formed against thee shall prosper. Isaiah 54 verse 17 When going threw thr storms when people throw darts at us we cry out to the Lord My grace is sufficient for thee for my strength is made perfect in weakness 2 Corinthians 12 verse 9 No matter what come your way God have are life in his hands your under God's protected shill Happy are those who are persecuted because they do what God reqires the Kingdom of heaven belongs to thim Happy are you when people insult you and persecute you and tell all kinds of evil lies against you because you are m y f ollwers be happy and glad, for a great reward is kept for you in heaven This is how the prophets who lived before you were persecuted. Matthew 5 verse 10-11 I will speak out to encourage Jerusalem I will not be silent until she is saved. Isaiah 62 verse 1 I hold you with my right hand I the Lord your God don't be afraid for I am here to help you. I chosen you and will not throw you away Isaiah 41 verse 9 When everything is ready. I will come and get you. So that you will always be with me where I am. John 14 verse 3 Israel you belong to me alone you were my sacred possession I sent suffering and disaster on everyone who hurt you I the Lord have spoken Jeremiah 2 verse 3 Trust in the Lord and do good, then land and prospen Bridle your anger trash your wrath cool your pipes it only makes things worse before long the crooks will be bankrupt god investors will soon own the store before you know it the wicked will have had it you' all stare at his once famous place and nothing down to earth people will move in and take over; relishing a huge bonaza believe on the word of god the truth Psalm 37 verse 8-910-11 Those who have been ransomed by the Lord will return but now Listen to this you afflicted ones who sit in drunken stupor though not from drinking wine. This is what the sovreign Lord your god and defender says see I have take the terrible cup from your hands you will drink no more of my fury. Instead will have that cup to your tormentors' those who said we will trample you into the dust and walk on your backs Isaiah 51 verse 11-21-22-23 The Lord said they are my people they will not deceive me and so he saved them. From all their suffering; It was not angel. But the Lord. Himself saved them in his love and compassion he rescued them. He had always taken care of them in the past. But they rebelled against him and make his holy spirit sad. So the Lord became their enemy and fought against them. But then they remembered the past the days of moses. The servant of the Lord and they asked. Where now is the Lord who saved the leaders of his spirit to Moses, where is the Lord. Who by his power did great things through moses. Dividing the waters of the sea and leading his people through the deep water, to win everlasting fame for himself Led by the Lord, they were as sure footed as wild horses. And never stumbled. As cattle are led into a fertile valley, So the Lord gave his people rest, he led his proplr and brought honor to his name. Isaiah 63 verse 8-910-11 Page 135 God make it plain in his word. For I know the plans I have for you say the Lord they are plans for good not for disaster to give you a future and hope If you look for me wholeheartedly you will find me I will be found by you says the Lord. I will end your cativity and restore your forunes. When c rcumstances, come the word of God always has a amswer to are everyday life Scriptures is the main goal to look for without God's word we will be lost in darkness When we go through trouble God is always in control when we go through trials. He will always place peace in are hearts When a man's ways please the Lord the Lord, he maketh even has his enemies to be at peace with him Proverbs 16 verse 7 and other Scriptures Bible Jeremiah 11 verse 13 if you obey the Lord you obey the lord your God and faithfully keep all his commands that I AM giving you today he will make you greater than any other nation on earth Obey the Lord your God and all these blessings will be yours But if you disobey the Lord your God and do not faithfully keep all his commands and laws that I am giving youy today, all these evil things will happen to you. Deuteronomy 28 verse 1-2-15 Ye adulterers and adulteresses know ye not that the friendship of the world is enmity with God? Whosoever therefore will be a friend of the world is the enemy of God. Don't think that there is, no truth in the scripture that says the spriit that God Placed in us is filled with fierce desires But the grace that God gives is even stronger as the scripture says, God resists the pround, but gives grace to humble James 4 verse 4-5-6 The Lord takes care of those who obey him Trust in the Lord and do Good. Live in the Land and be safe, PSALM 37 verse 2-18 What a joy it is to find just the right word for the right occasion Proverb 15 verse 23 and the land will be their forever Psalm 37 verse 19 Joyful are those who listen to me. Watching for me daily at my gates. Waiting for me outside my home For whoever finds me finds life and receives favor from the Lord. But those who miss me injure themselves, all who hate me love death, that's Proverbs 8 verse 34-35 I yes, I am the Lord and there is no other savior Frist I predicted your rescue then I saved you and proclaimed it to the world from eternity to eternity I am God. No one can snatch anyone out of my hand, no one can undo what I have done, Isaiah 43 verse 11 You will have courage because you will have hope. Job 11 verse 18 she won his favor Esther 2 verse 17 Before talking about the word we need read the guidance of God word and every day life. He will be our guide even to the end, Psalm 48-14 Page 136 For the Lord your God is amerciful God he will not abandon you or destroy you or forget the solema covenant he made with your ancestors. Deuteronomy 3 verse 31 how great is the goodness you have stored up for those who fear you. You lavish it on those who come to you for protection. Psalm 31 verse 19 blessing them before the watching world. You hide them in the shelter of your presence safe from those who conspire against them you shelter them in your presence far from accusing tongues praise the Lord. For he has shown me the wonders of his unfailing love. He kept me safe when my city was under attack. In panic I cried out, I am cut off from the Lord. But you heard my cry for mercy and answered my call for help, love the lord, all you godly ones foe the lord protects those who are loyal to him. That is why we must hold all the more firmly to the truth we have heand so that we will not br carried away Hebrews 2 verse 1 come back to the Lord your God. He is kind and full of mercy he is patient and keeps his promise he is always ready to forgive and not punish. Joel 2 verse 13 Now I am going to give you. Grain and wine and olive oill. And you will be satsfed Joel 2 verse 19 Who has done wonderful things for you. My people wil never be despised again. You will praise the Lord your God who has done wonderful thang for you. Jeoel 2 verse 26-27 Then Israel you will know that I am among you and that I the Lord am your God and there no other my people will never be dispised again, Y ou are coming to Chist who is the living corner stone of God's temple. He was rejected by people but he was chosen by God for great honor. I Peter 2 verse 4-5 And you are living stones that God is building into his spiritual temple what's more you are his holy priests through the medition of Jesue Christ you offer spirtual sarifiles that please God Page 137 Consider it pure joy. My brothers when ever you face trials of many kinds because you know that the testing of your faith develops perseverance James 1 verse 2-4 Perseverance must finishits work so that you may be maturs and complet not lacking anything. Be good to your servant that I may live and obey your word. Psalm 119 verse 17 But as for you, be strong and do not give up for your work will be rewarded 2 Chronicles in won the chapter These were all commended for their faith yet none of them received what had been promised. God had planned something better for us so that only together with us would they be made perfect Hebrews 11 verse 11 how I want to be there I LONG TO BE IN THE Lord's temple. With my whole being I sing for joy to the living God. How happy are those who live in your temple always singing praise to you. Psalm 84 verse 2-4 Psalm 84 verse 11 for the Lord God is a sun and shield: the Lord will give grace and glory: no good thing will he withhold from them that walk up rightly. No good thing will he with hold from them that uprightly we mark by God Let us walk honestly as in rioting and drunkeness not in chambering and wantonness not in strife and envying Romans 13 verse 13 pure religion and undefiled before God and the father is this to vist the fatherless and widows in their affiction and to keep himself unspotted dfrom the world James 1 verse 27 Page 138 Philippians 4 verse 13 I can do all things through Christ who strengthens me. Psalm 56 verse 10 I praise God for what he has promised yes. I praise the Lord for what he has promised. Verse 11 I trust in God so why should what can mere mortals do to me. Isaiah 45 verse 24 the people will declare the Lord is the cource of all my righteousness and strength and all who were angry with will come to him and be ashamed. Verse 25 in the Lord all the generations of Israel will be justified and in him they will boast, the name of the Lord is a strong fortress the godly run to him and are safe, Provrbs 18 verse 10 Rejoice in our confident hope be patient in trouble and keep on praying. When God's people are in need be ready to help them always be eager to practice hospitality. Romans 12 verse 15 Isaiah 30 verse 15 This is what the sovereign lord, the holy one of Israel says only in returing to me and resting in me will you be saved in quietness and confidence is your strength but you would have none of it verse 18 So the Lord must wait for you to come to him so he can show you his love and compassions for the Lord is a faithful God. Blessed are those who wait for his help. Verse 19 o people of zion who live in Jerusalem, you will weep no more, he will be gracious if you ask for help. He will surely respond sound of your crieas, Because you trusted me. I will give you life as a rewars I will rescue you and keep you safe I the Lord have spoken. Jeremiah 40 verse 18 keep busy with the eternal one by obeying God by concerned above everything else with the Kingdom of God and with what he requires of you, and he will provide you with all these other things, Matthew 6 verse 33 Give to worried to God complaining don't help. seek the Lord and prayer and aks God for help. lots of people in the world go threw dispersion every day of the year more people end of killing they self or on drugs or drink to. about a billon people each day because they don't have Jesue in they live they have no hope in they life with out God there no voild in life to fill. Or some may have a nurvirse break down. They know God, but they do not give him the honor that belongs to him, nor do they thank him. Instead, their thoughts have become complet nonsense, and their empty minds are filled with darkness. They say they are wise, but they are fools; instead of worshiping the immortal God, they worship images made to look like mortals or birds or animals or reptiles. And God has given those people over to do the filthy things their hearts desire, and they do shameful things with each other. They exchange the truth about God for a lie; they worship and serve what God has created in stead of the Creator himself, who is to be praised forever Amen. Because they do this, God has given them over to shameful pasion. Even the women pervert the natural acts. In the same way the men give up natural sexual relations with women and burn with passion for each other Men do shameful things with each other, and as a result they bring upon themselves the punishment they deserve for their wrongdoing. Because those people refuse to keep in mind the true knowledge about God, he has given them over to corrupted minds, so that they do the things that they should not do. They are filled with all kinds of wickedness, evil, greed, and vice; they are full of jealousy, murder. Fighting, deceit, and malice. They g ossip and speak evil of one another. They are hateful to God, insolent, proud, and boastful. They think of more ways to do evil they disobey their parents, they have no conscience they do not keep their promises, and they show no kindness or pity for others, They know that God's law says that serve death. Yet not only do they continue to do these very things, but they even approve of others who do them. Romans 1 VERSE 21-22-23-24-25-26-27-28-29-30-31 Page 140 Then the Lord came down in a cloud and stood there with him. And he called out his own name. Yahweh the Lord the God of compassion and mercy I am slow to anger and filled with unfaling love fanithfulness. I lavish unfailing love and faithfulness. I lavish unfailing love to a thousand generations, and forgive evil and sin but I will not fail to punish children and grandchildren to the third and fourth genrration for the sin of their parents," Exodus 34 verse 7 Moses quickly bowed down to the ground and worshiped he said Lord if you really are pleased with me I ask you to go with us. These people are stubborn, but forgive our evil and our sin, and accept us as your own people. Exodus 34 verse 8 Don't be afraid he said take courage I am here, Mark 6 verse 50 if God be for us who can be against us, Romans 8 verse 31 here is God's answer to every guestion of fear. Certainly I will be with you no matter what guestion you may have if you know that God is with you. You need not fear Exodus 3 verse 11 I yes I am the Lord, and there is no other savior. Frist I predicted your rescue then I saved you and proclaimed it to the world. No foreign god has ever done this you are witness that I am the only God. Says the Lord. From eternity to eternity I am God, no one can snatch anyone out of my hand. No one can undo what I have done. Isaiah 43 verse 11-12-13 Fear not you will no longer live in shame Don't be afraid there is no more disgrace for you, Isaiah 54 verse 4 So he himself stepped in to save them with his strong arm, Isaiah 59 verse 16 He was Stepped in to save them with his strong arm and his justice sustained him. He put on rightewsness as his body armor and placed the helmet of salvation on his head he clothed himself with a robe of vengeance and wrapped himself in a cloak of divine passion. He will repay his enemies for their evil deeds Isaiah 59 verse 16-17-18 All nations will come to your light mighiy kings will come to see your radiance. The descendants of your tormenters will come and bow before you. Those who despised you will kiss your feet. They will call you the city of the Lord the zion of thr holy one of Israel, Though you were once despised and hated, with no traveling through you. I will make you beautiful forever, a joy to all generations, powerful kings and mighty nations will satisfy your every need, as though you were a child nursing at the breast of a queen. You will know at last that I the Lord, am your redeemer the mighty one of Israel. Iwill exchange your bronze for gold your iron for silver your wood for bronze and your stone for iron. I will make peace your leader and righteousness your ruler. Violence will disappear from your land. The desolion and destruction of war will end. Salvation will surround you like city walls and praise will be on the lips of all who enter there No longer will you need the sun to shine by day nor the moon to give its light by night for the Lord your God will be your everlasting light and your God will be your glory. Isaiah 60 verse 13-14-15-16-17-18-19 My Personal Story, way back in the days when I was going up I met this man we no each other since way back. I come to find out he was pipe and a drung added he try to have me to belive he was a good person but he was not nice at all. his communication was not right with me at all I try to tell Joe that's his name is not the way to live telling what God Says in the bible. Thou shalt not kill Deuteronomy 4 verse 17 But you belong to God my chidren, and have defeated the false prophets, because the spirit who is in you is more powerful than the spirit in those who belong Those false prophets speak about matters of the world, and the world listens to them because they belong to the world. But we belong to God. Whoever knows God listens to us whoever does not belong to God does not listen to us, this then is how we can tell the difference between the Spirit of truth and the spirit of error. 1 John 4 verse 4 I made bad choice being with him finalley I let him go I handle the problem the only way I no how to do We know that no children of God keep on sinning, for the Son of God keeps them safe, and the evil one cannot harm them, We know that we belong to God even thought the whole world. Is under the rule of the evil one We know that the Son of God has come and has given us understanding. So that we know the true God We live in union with his Son Jesue Christ This is the true God, and this is eternal life. My children keep yourselves safe from false god's, 1John 5 verse 20 Page 141 My handling the Problem. By praying and reading the word of God and obeying his will for the day and not look back what you did and the past is not necessary. but focus on your further is yet to come. We all make mistakes none of us not prefect But we serve a perfect God, by making mistakes make us a better person. We must not look back. No man, having put his hand to the plow. And looking back. Is fit for the kingdom of God. Luke 10 verse 62 Jesus answered, Verily verily I say unto thee Except a man be born of water and of the Spirit he cannot enter into the kingdom of God That which is born of the flesh is flesh and that which is born of the spirit is spirit John 2 verse 3 Like a example you got to chance your hole life stly by being Christ like we should not be frinds with the wicked Love must be completely sincers. Hate what is evil, on what is good. Love one another warmly as Christians, and be eager to show respect for one another Work hard and do not belazy. Serve the Lord with a heart full of devotion, Let your hope keep you joyful be patient in your troubles, and pray at all times, Share your belongings with your needy fellow Christians, and open your homes to strangers. Ask God to bless those who persecute you-yes, ask him to bless, not to curse. Be happy with those who are happy, weep with those who are happy, weep with those who weep.

Have the same concern for everyone. Do not be proud, but accept humble duties, do not think of yourselves wise. If someone has done you wrong, do not repay him with a wrong. Try to do what everyone considers to be good. Do everything possible on your part to live in peace with everybody Never take revenge my friends, but instead let God's anger do It. For the scripture says, "I will take revenge, instead. As the scripture says if your enemies are hungry feed them if they are thirsty give them a drink for by doing this you will make them burn with shame Do not let evil defeat you instead conquer evil with good, Romans 12 verse 11-12-13-14-15-16-17-18-19-20-21 You will keep in perfect peace all whose thoughts are fixed on you, trust in the lord God is the eternal rock. Isaiah 26 verse 3 He humbles the proud and brings down the arrogant city he brings it down to the dust the poor and oppressed trample it under foot. And the needy walk all over it. Isiah 26 verse 5 verse 6-7 But for those who are righteous. The way is not steep and rough. You are a God who does what is right and you smooth out the patch ahead of them, verse 8 Lord we show our trust in you by obeying your laws our heart's desire is to glorify your name, all night long I search for you in the morning I earnestly seek for God for only when you come to judge the earnesty seek for God. For only when you come to judge the earth will people learn what is right. The wicked keep doing wrong. And take no notice of the Lord majesty verse 11 O Lord they pay no attention to your upraised fist. Show there your eager ness to defend your people then they will be ashamed. Let your fire consume your enemies, verse 12 Lord. You will grant us peace. All we have accomplished is really from you. Verse 13 O Lord our God others have rulled us, but you alone are the one we worship. Those we served before are dead and gone, their departed spirits will never return. Page 142 PAGE 109 Before talking about the word we need to read the guidance of God's word and are every day life, Psalm 48 verse 14 He will be our guide even to the end NLT BIBLE whether in Difficuhies I made a decision to have a spiritual walk with Jesue to develop a guide to changed how live according to God's will thought hard times facing struggle and circumstances in my life Jouney my Hope is in God, he is the only help I no who allways keeps his promises he never fell me yet Regardless what going on I will succeed all my goals in Life. But they that wait upon the Lord shall renew their strength. They shall mount up with wings as eagles; they shall run and not be weary and they shall walk and not faint, Isaiah 40 verse 31 My Lord has Favor on me he persevere me before the foundation of the word I had lots of battle in my life But God had me cover everstept of the way Even I was not walking right some days or not obeying God like I should But God is helping me each stept everyday of my life, Even today he my spiritual guide coach coaching me and the right Directions, Genesis 28 verse 15 What's more, I am with you, and I will protect you wherever you go, Jesue is my Leader I will obey his commands and be delight in his teacheing and his directions to way to go as he spoke the word of God in every generation still yet to come. Look for the Rainbow why you are out side, Possibility will take time on God's timeing not on are time But the Lord time we will reseed hope from God promises when not looking for are breakthrew that's are surprise just like one your friends throw you a party and when you walk in the room when you not looking when you turn on the lights and all of that monment everything change and right in front of you, and you being praying and wishing for that birtday party surprise you want it for years but no one had the resoure to plan the surprise birthday party and you findly forget and think no more about it and that day God Rememberance because you trust and Pray and let it go And God already took care of the production and had all ready schedule the appointment suddenly your whole life circumstances is a new beganing for you life, Jeremiah 31-16-17 There is hope for your Futhre says the Lord. When take to the Lord in prayer and let it go of your breaktrew regardless how long it may take place keep praying until God answer your prayer thangs will changed over night it will happened. When you have a Assignment God not gone let's you miss your postions your Appointment is already on schedle God got you on his report before you even call he already answer your prayer, In those days when you pray I will listen. If you look for me wholeheartedly you will find me I will be found by you says the Lord. I will end your captivity and restore your fortunes, I sent you and will bring you home again to your own land. Jeremiah 29 verse12-13 Page 110 Mental Health Recovery.

All my life I been going threw mental illness shy uncomfortable Very Emotions all of time worried and feeling bad down but not out by Education my self by going to mental health programs to help other to let them no there is hope in God out there if I can get well they can too I would like to be an Leadership some day by supporting the community to let them no there help out there when you going threw mental Prolems, People with Disabilities are people to they are Human being are going trew bad times too and they can make a diffent to others as well with provided medsion for your health and seeing your doctor on Regurlar basis you will be ok. By doing are part we can make a difffent, I am recovery from Schizophrenic I had for 20 years, I doing much better stronger and wiser and God give me the stenght today and everyday of my life I have a lots of support other people and my family as well with love and kindness now I doing good Now keep my self in ministries in the missshing filll and take time to help others when I go trew everyday, I take one stept of the time each day on my jouney on my everyday life, I spen more time with God well try too. Page 111 I have a positive aattitude about my self I believe God and his will for my life should be fulfilled faith in my Lord by study the word of God and practicing in his present helps my progress by keeping me strong when I weak Praying is the main key of Life especially on my bad days and when going therw miserable problem and emotions hurting even I don't unstand I Still trust God my promotion will take place one day the glory of God answer a coming change already been spokek 2 Corinthians 3 verse 18 But we all with open face beholding as in a glass the glory of the lord are changed into the same image from glory to glory even as by the spirt of the lord, Romans 3 verse 23 For all have sinned, and come short of the glory of God; verse 24 Being justified freely by his grace through the redemption that is in Christ Jesus, Mark 9 verse 9 And he said unto them verily I say unto you, That there be some of them that stand here, which shall not taste of death till they have seen the kingdom of God come with power, Revelation 21 verse 12 and behold I come quickly, and my reward is with me to give every man according as his work shall be verse 13 I am Alpha and Omega the beginning and the end the First and the last I am Looking forward for a brighter future but I believe what I Receive When I have good memories What God did for me I praise the lord anyhow, Get all the Advice you can and you will succeed without it you will fail what a joy it is to find just the right word for the right occasion, Proverbs 15 verse 23 The Love of God By a pastor the love of God is with you in grace and peace in time of trouble and turmal remember nothing can separate us from the love of God-this is peace in the midst of the storm, Genesis 18 verse 14 is Anything too hard for the Lord Jeremiah 31 verse 37 There is hope for your future," says the Lord. Joshua 1 verse 5 no one will be able to stand against you as long as you live, for I will be with you as I was with mosese, I will not fell you or abandon you. Verse 8 study this book of instruction continually, mediate on it day and night so you will be sure to obey everything written in it only then will you [prosper and succed in all you do, verse 9 This my Command be strong and courageous do not be afraid or discouraged for the Lord your God is with you wherever you go, My God keeps his word when he said it, it should be done, The Lord is very good to me on my jouney today he bless my plans to be perfect all threw the day and he's not gone leave this far and leave me by my self now. he has everything under control I will not quit on my Lord And Jesue will not quit on me. So why do I complain or worried because God will be there quik fast and an hurry So I thank carefully and positive when I going threw struggle I no G od will be there on the double and he restore my trouble, Page 112 Don't pick on people, jump on their failures, criticize their faults unless, of course, you want the same treatment, don't condemn those who are down; that hardness can boomerang, Luke 6 verse 37-38 T MB, Be easy on people you'll find life a lot easier, Give away your life; you'll find like given back. But not merely given back-given back bonus and blessing, giving. Not getting, is the way.

Generosity begets genersity all my life people treat me like garbage those people came at me like a whirl wind But God help every step of the way when I going threw storms I completely give it to God in prayer, when some one do you wrong they do nothing but hurting they self because they the one will fail not you I will bless those who bless you and curse those who treat you with contempt. Genesis 12 verse 3 back in my past my exboy friend use me even he told me he was using me, he realey hurt me Rorbert Would ask me for surgar and stamps and want a plate of food and envelopes and menesion And money every time he called he won't something almost everyday he was a pain in the but, see he live two doors dowm from me were I stay. One day I put a stop to that, he tole he got married Con to find out he never was devoice he had me to believe he was not married, and Bob got the nurve ask for help again I tole him that's not my consern that's you and your wife responsibilities don't come to my house again when you see me just say hi and keep stepping you not wellcome here, then days past I herd Robert lost everything H e want back were he came from back in the dumps what he did to me boomerang right back on him I herd he want rock boton his griendfriend he was with at the time she made a dumbie out of him and kick him to the curve I dump Bob at the time because he wanted to be with stacy so I set him free after he beg me back 3 times to take him back so said ok like a dummy and very same day Rortbert call stacy right in front of me like I was to dum to nodise asking her to come over his house this weeking, after he got to talking to her I did speek for while then I said to Bob if you want to be with Stacy that's find with me I will never being your Women not now ever again for now on we just be friends you mess are relationship we will never be no connecting not now or forever even his own wife don't want noting to do with him that's what he get for trying to get over on people you don't get good come to you wen you try get over on somebody, Luke 37 verse38 Don't condemn those who who are down that hardness can boomerang. Be easy on people you'll life a lot easier, As look toward the window think of the memories what God broght out today I did say no compaing word out my mouth God show up what had happened I went out today to take care some business and have got done early my ride could not come wrigth then A very nice old lady over herd me talk on the phone and she was concern about me getting home she started to talk to me abound her life story and I listen to her and courange her and pray with her about God and telling her don't worried God will take care of you Philippians 4 verse 19 And this same God who take care of me will supply all your needs from his glorious riches, which have been given to us in Christ Jesue. I telling her What the scritpure In the bible AND ALLSO G od not gone leave you this far and lafe you by your selfe now Just think what he broth you from in your past you made it then and you willl make it now I was saying to her don't worry about God have you cover, I was couraging miss bee think positive toward her future. Page 113 Mark 10 verse 27 without God. Is utterly impossible But with God everything is possible, who I say, love your enemies pray for those who persecute you. In that way, you will be acting as true children of your Father in heaven. For he gives his sunlight to both the evil and the good, and he sends rain on the just and the unjust alike if you love only those who love you, what reward is there for that Even corrupt tax collectors do that much. If you are kind only to your friends. How are you different from anyone else, Even pagans do that. But you are to be perfect even your Father in heaven is perfect, Matthew 5 44-45-46-47-48 So many storms today I had to spen more time with God my enemies do me so wrong but God keep me strong they had no respect for me what so ever they treat me like a animal like I am a out cast they made my Reputation look bad I no some thing was said about me by my others enemies with false information. I be glad when the Lord pulll the covers off them Jon Frankie Leann and Lucy and Jim and they potsey they did me wrong and try to still make me look like public disgrace. When I have God on my side I can't lose Isaiah 59 verse 15 the Lord looked and was displeased to find there was no justice, verse 16 He was amazed to see that no one intervend to help the oppressed so he himself stepped in to save them with his strong arm, verse 17 And his justice sustained him he put on righteousness as his body armor and placed the helmet of savation on his head he clothed himself with robe of vengeance and wrapped himself in a cloak of divine passion he will repay his enemies for their evil deeds, the good bible allways provid me good information applies to me and God people who go threw storms and whirl wind when are enemies give us a hard time, Never the less he saved them for his name's sake that he might make his mighty power to be known. Psalm 106 verse 8 they will fight against you like an attacking arny, but I will make you as secare as a fortified wall of bronze they will not conquere you, I the Lord have spoken, yes, I will certainly keep you safe from these wicked men, Jeremiah 15 verse 20-21 and Jesue said But don't be afraid of those who threaten you for the time is coming when everything that is covered will be revealed, and all that is secret will be made know to all What I tell you now in the darkness, shout abroad when daybreak comes, what I whisper in your ear, shout from the housetops for all to hear, Mattrhew 10 verse 26-27 Fear not you will no longer live in shame. Don't be afraid. There is no more disgrace for you. You wil no longer rember the shame of youth, Isaiah 54 verse 4-17 But in that coming day no weapon turned against you will succeed Yes I will certainly keep you safe from these wicked men, I will resue you from their cruel hands," Jermiah 15 verse 21 I see that the Lord is always with me. I will not be shaken, for he is right beside me, no wonder my heart is glad and my tongue shouts his praises; my body rest in hope Acts 2-25-26 Page 114 Obey the Lord your God and all these blessing will be yours, Deuteronomy 28 verse 2 But straight way Jesus spake unto them, saying Be of Good cheer it I be not afraid. Matthew 14 verse 27 on my Journey I had to educate my sefe and make a appointment with God everday of my life by praying and reading the word of God because deep down in me I was not doing right or living right for God I was bitter mad mean and hirt but I still trust Jesue to help me eveystept of the way., if I say. My foot slips, your mercy, O Lord will hold me up. Psalm 94-18 Oh Lord help me please give me the strength, I would say it my on my daily regularly basices, I look at the sky and a Rainbow is in the air That God letting me no he keeps his promies for me There is hope in God. Every time I see that Rainbow in that sky I no God keeps his covenant. Then God said, I am giving you a sign of my covenant with you and with all living creatures, for all generations to come, I have place my rainbow in the clouds. It is the sign of my covenant with all the earth, Genesis 8 verse 12-13 All Believers come here and listen, let me tell you what God did for me, I called out to him with my mouth, my tongue shaped the sounds of music, if I had been cozy with evil the Lord would never have listened, But he most surely did listen, he came on the double when he heard my prayer, Blessed be God he didn't turn a deaf ear, he stayed with me, loyal in his love, Luke 4 verse 43 I must preach the good news of the kingdom of God in other towns, too because that is why I was sent. I had a good day today when I go out front of the public in the community were there different programs I get to Shair the gospel about Christ by the way I act with love and kindness and supporting them when they are going threw decision on there recovery from different season threw life, In my church out reach hospital and family and others are in need of help that my assignment to educad other people let them no there a hope and a chance and a season that God has a appointment time for are day for a braektrew you have to been trew to help others where they are going trew right now. God is able to take care of you his love will never end. Neither death nor life neither angels nor demons neither the present nor the future nor any powers neither heigh nor depth, nor anything else in all creation will be able to separate us from the love of God that is in Christ Jesus our Lord. Romans 8 verse 38-39 This is what the Lord says your Redeemer, the Holy one of Israel, I am the Lord your God who teaches you what is good for you and leads you along the paths you should follow Never can a Mother forget her nusing child she has borne. But ever if that were possible, I would not forget you. I have written your name on the palms of my hands, As surely as I live says the Lord they will be like jewels or bridal ornaments for you to display Isaiah 49 verse 15-16-`18 This is what the sovereign Lord says; see, I will give a signal to the godless nations. They will carry your little sons back to you in their arms. Verse 22 They will bring your daughters on their shoulders, verse23 Kings and queens will serve you and care for all your needs. They will bow to the earth before you and lick the dust from your feet, then you will know that I am the Lord, Those who trust in me will never be put to shame, The King speaks with divine authority his Decisions are always right, Proverbs 16 nerse 10 I will give up whole nations to save your life because you are preious to me and because I love you and give you honor, Do not be afraid I am with you. I saiah 43 verse 4 Regardless what we going threw struggle in are everyday circumstances God have a word for us for the day we will succeed will be a possibility hope absolutely chance take place in are future says the Lord. There is hope for your future says the Lord Jer emiah 31 verse 16-17 there hope for people with mental illnes and other people as well because we have a facvor of God on are life are condition will be hill by the promise HE don't lie God is not a man, that he should lie; neither the son of man. That he should repent; hatch he said. And shall he not do it or hath he spoken, and shall he not make it good/ Behold I have received commamdment to bless; and he hath not beheld iniqity in ja-cob neither hath he seen perverseness in is-rael the lord his God is with him and the shout of a king is among them Numbers 23 verse 19-20 Page 114 Isaiah verse 8 the Lord says I love justice and I hate oppression and crime, I will faithfully reward my people, an make an eternal covenant with them verse 9 they will be famous among the nations, everyone who sees them will know that they are a people whom I have blessed. I going threw suffering but God is still is in control I still prass him no matter what happen My God will saved me I have to stay strong by God grace I can make it he will answer my prayer in his time, The Lord said they are my people they will not deceive me, and so he saved them from all their suffering it was not an angel, but the Lord himself who saved them in his love and compassion he rescued them he had always take care of them in the past Isaiah 63 verse 8 Obey the Lord your God and all these blessings will be yours Deuteronomy 28 verse 2 B ut if you disobey the Lord your God and and do not faithfully keep all his commands and laws that I am giving you today, all these evil things will happen to you verse 15 if we don't obey God And we be unfaithful we will run in all kind bad luck so we must obey God by fasting and praying and going to the Trone of grace by reading his word at all times. unfaithful people don't you know that to be the worlds friend means to be God's enemy Don't think that there is no truth in the scripture that says the spririt that God placed in us is filled with fierce desires, But the grace that God gives is even stronger, as the scripture says, God resists the proud, but gives grace to the humble James 4 verse 4 The Lord take care of those who obey him. Psalm 37 verse 18

Psalm 37 verse 2 Trust in the Lord and do good live the land and be safe, But seek ye first the kingdom of God and his righteousness; and all these things shall be added unto you Matthew 6 verse 33 I have to think postitive about life. I am very happy to be here this moring alive and well my God came threw for me again he woke me up and start my day fresh, I think the lord for a nuther day thank you Jesue I acknowledged your name with a hard of thankgiving I thankful for a new hope and your grace for the day I thank you o Lord for a great day, help me to have patient and have a peace in the Love of Christ in me and my family as well, help us not to give up in trow in the towel. I no we will still win the victory because we got you Jesue on are side I am glade you chose us to be your servants we not perfect but we serve a perfect God. Psalm 41 verse 12 you have preserved my live because I am innocent you have brought me into your prsence forever, verse 13 praise the Lord, the God of Israel who lives from everlasting to everlasting amen and amen,. Jeremiah 29 verse 11 for I know the plans I have for you say the Lord they are for good and not for disaster to give you a future and a hope the faithful love of the Lord never ends his mercies never cease, great is his faithfulness his mercies begin afresh each moring I say to myself the Lord is my inheritance. Therefore I will hope in him, Lamentations 3 verse23-24-25 the Lord is good to those who depend on him to those who search for him, verse26 so it is good to wait guiety for salvation from the Lord verse 31 for no one is abandoned by the Lord forever, verse 33 for he does not enjoy hurting people or causing them sorow Lamentations 3 verse 40 in stead let us test and examine our ways, let us turn back to the lord, verse 41 let us lift our heart and hands to God in heaven and say we have sinned and rebelled and you have not forgiven us, verse 55 But I called on your name. Lord from deep within the pit you heard me when I cried listen to my pleading verse 57 hear my cry for help yes, you came when I called you told me do not fear verse 58 Lord you are my lawyer plead my case for you have redeemed my life you have seen the wrong they have done to me Lord Be my judge and prove me right, verse 4 Pay them back Lord for all the evil they have done give them hard and stubborn hearts, and then let your curse fall on them Luke 6 verse 35 But love ye your enemies and do good and lend hoping for nothing again and your reward shall be great, we sure focus on eternal life not the things of the world having your mine on jesus is the number one thing to do pay attention to God not your problems take it to the Lord in prayer keep your mine on Christ by reading the word of God or sharing Jesue with other unbelievers who need or want are help some will not receive what you say about God word here what God says in the bible And whosoever shall not receive you. Nor hear your words when ye depart out of that house or city shake off the dust of your feet. Matthew 10 verse 14 And Je'-sus came and spake unto them, saying All power is given unto me in heaven and in earth. Go ye therefore, and teach all nations, baptizing them in the name of the Father, and of the son, and of the Holy Ghost; Teaching them to observe all things, whatsoever I have commanded you; and I am with you always, even unto the end of the world A-men. Matthew 28 verse 18-19-20 Follow me. John 21 vers 19 No man can serve two masters; for either he will hate the one, and love other, Ye cannot serve God and mam-mon Matthew 6 verse 25 Page 115 Don't become partners with these who reject God, how can you make a partnership out of righr and wrong. That;s not parthership that's war is light best friends with dark does Christ go strolling with the devil do trust and mistrust hold hands. Who would think of pagan idols in God's holy temple, But that exactly what we are each of us a temple in whom God lives, God himself put it this way, I'll live in them move into them, I'll be their John 16-13 God will do this for he says, and he has invited you into partnership with his his son, Jesus Christ our Lord, 1 CORINTHIANS IN ONE OF THE VERSE. And God also says in the word This then is the message which we have heard of him and declare unto you, that God is light, and in him is no darkness at all. If we say that we have fellowship with him, and walk in darkness, we lie, and do not the truth 1 John verse 5-6 vers 7 But if we walk in the light as he is in the light, we have fellowship one with another, and the blood of Jesus Christ his son cleanseth us from all sin, Taste and see that the Lord is good; oh the joy of those who take refuge in him; fear the Lord, you his godly people. For those who fear the lord you his godly people, for those who fear him will have all they need Psalm 34 verse 8-9 All praise to God, the father of our Lord Jesus christ. It is by his great mercy that we have been born again, because God raised Jesue christ from the dead, now we live with great expectation verse 4 and we have a priceless inheritance-an inheritance that is kept in heaven for you, pure and undefiled, Beyond the reach of change and decay. And his power until you receive this salvation which is ready to be revealed on the last day for all to see, So be truly glad there is wonderful joy ahead, even though you have to endure many trials for a little while, These trials will show that your faith is genuine, It is being tested as fire test and purifies gold though your faith is far more precious than mere gold, So when your faith remains strong through many trials, it will bring you much praise and glory and honor on the day when Jesus christ is revealed to the whole word you love him even though you have never seen him though you do not see him now, you trust him. With a glorious inexpressible joy. The reward for trusting him. Will be the salvation of your souls. This salvation was something even the prophets wanted to know more about when they prophesied about this gracious salvation prepared for you. They wondered what time or situation the spirit of christ within them was talking about when he told them in advance about Christ's suffering and his great glory They were told that their message were not for themselves but for you, and now this good news has been announced to you by those who preached in the power of the holy spirit sent from heaven. It is all so wonderful that even the angels are eagerly watching these things happen, So think clearly and exercise self-control. Look forward to the gracious salvation that will come to you when Jesus Christ is revealed to the world. So you must live as God's obedient childred don't slip back unto your old ways of living to satisfy your own desires. You didn't know any better then, but now you must be holy in everything you do, just as God. Who chose you is holy for the scriptures say. You must be holy because I am holy. And remember that the heavenly father to whom you pray has no favorites, he will judge or reward you according to what tou do so you must live in reverent fear of him during your time as foreigners in the land, for you know that God paid a ransom to save you from the empty life you in herited from your ancestors, and the ransom he paid was not mere gold or silver. Spotless lamb of God. God chose him as your ransom long before the world began, but he has now revealed him to you in these last days, through Christ you have come to trust in God and you have placed your faith and hope in God because he raised Christ from the dead and gave him great glory. You were cleansed from your sins when you obeyed the truth. So now you must show sincere love to each other as brothers and sisters. Love each other deeply with all your heart for you have been born again but not to a life that will quickly end. Your new life will last forever because it comes from the eternal living word of God. As the scriptures say. People are like grass their beauty is like a flower in the field, the grass withers and the flower fades but the word of the Lord remains and that's word is the Good News that was preached to you. Page 117 1Peter1 verse 3-4-5-6-7-8-9-10-11-12-13-14-15-16-17-18-19-20-21-Romans 10 verse 10 for it is by our faith that we are put right with God it is by our confession that we are saved so then faith come from hearing the message comes through preaching Christ. And Jesus concluded listeten, then if you have ears verse 17 today Salvation by God reached me threw Grace because I obey Jesue I am going threw all Circumstances But Still I Trust God in my trouble my example being connect to a Relationship with God means give my all to him I don't always worship like I should but I will try to go back to my daily visited to reached the throme of mercy and grace Jesue answered, the knowledge about the secrets of the kingdom of heaven has been given to you but not to them for the person who has something will be given more so that he will have more than enough but the person who has nothing will have taken away from him even the little he has the reason I use parables in taking to them is that they look, but do not see, and they listen, but do not hear or understard So the prophecy of Isaiah applies to them, this people will listen and listen but not understand they will look and look but not see because their minds are dull, and they have stopped up their ears and have closed their eyes otherwise their eyes would see, their ears would hear their minds would understand and they would turn to me. Says God and I would heal them, as for you how fortunate you are your eyes see and your ears hear I assure you that many prophets and many of God's people wanted very much to see what you see, but they could not and to hear what you hear, but they did not Listen then and learn what the parable of the sower means, those who hear the message about the kingdom but do not understand it are like the seeds that fell along the evil one come and snatches away what was sown in them the seeds that fell on rocky ground stand for those who receive the message gladly as soon as they hear it but it does not sink deep into them and they don't last long so trouble or persecution comes because of the message they give up at once, the seeds that fell among thron bushes stand for those who hear the message, but the worries about this life and the love for riches choke the message and they don't bear fruit and the seeds sown in the good soil stand for those who hear the message and understand it they bear fruit some as much as one hundred. Other sixty and others thirty Matthew 13 verse 11 12-13-14 threw20-21-22-23 Remember this my dear friends everyone must be quick to listen but slow to speak and slow to become angry. 2 Timothy 2 verse 1 take the teachings that you heard me proclaim in the presence of many witnesses and entrust them to reliable people who will be able to teach others also, That's is why we must hold on all the more firmly to the truth we have heard so that we will not be carried away Hebrews 2 verse1 are you listen to God he speaking to you obey and here what he saying to you Page 118 God is not a man so he does not lie he is not human, so he not change his mind. Has he ever spoken and failled to act has he ever promised and not carried through. Numbers 23 verse 19 5 STEPT to you with your prayer life. 1 Important to allways walk with God at all times listen Jesue will respond oh Lord help me to pay attention and worshipt Matthew 6 verse 33 instead be concerned above everything else with the kingdom of God and with what he reqires of you, and he will provide you with all these other things. GNTB. STEPT 2 Hebrews 13 verse 5 he hath said I will never leave thee nor for sake thee. Believe in the possible. Philippian 1 verse 4 Always in every prayer of mine for you all making request with joy, verse 5 for your fellowship in the gospel from the first day until now, verse 6 being confident of this very thing, that he which hatch begun a good work in you will perform it until the day of Jesue Christ, is by stating now to have fellowship with God ask Jesue in life right now he take you as you are repent. Ask God in your life and save me for Jesus sake and asks the Lord what to do. STEPT 3 Regardless what going on in your life ether you have a bad day or a good day even you don't understand obey and trust Jesue in your jouney everyday life. Mark 10 verse 27 without God it is utterly impossible but with God everything is possible Psalm 46 verse 10 Be still, and know that I am God. I will be honored by every nation I will be honored throng out the world. STEPT 4 Wait on God. To take care of the circumstances Progress has all been provide with out delay God have you cover you. your bless by the best. Genesis 18 verse 14 anything too hard for the Lord. STEPT 5 Proverbs 8 verse 34 Joyful are those who listen to me, watching for me daily at my gates, watching for me outside my home, verse 35 for whoever finds me finds life and receives favor from the Lord But those who miss me injure themselves all who hate me love death, John 12 verse 46 I have come into the world as light. So that everyone who believes in me should not remain in the darkness verse 47 if people hear my message and not obey it, I will not judge the world, but to save verse 48 Those who reject me and do not accept my message have one who will judge them. The words I have spoken will be the judge on the last days verse 49 This is true, because I have not spoken on my own authority But the father has told me. My journey for the day God is precious to me he will be always my frist love in my life Psalms 36 verse 7 How precious, o God, is your constant love we find protection under the shadow of your wings. We feast on the abundant food you provide; you let us drink from the river of your goodness. Today was A great day Everything thing work out according to God's plan I had my good days and my bad days But God Response to my prayer Every chance he get when I call on God he answer Psalm 91 verse 15 When they call on me. I will answer. I will be with them in trouble. 2 Corinthians verse 8 my grace is all you need. My power works best in weakness, I will rescue and honor them. Verse 16 I will reward them with a long life and give them my salvation. I was going threw all kind of troubles but God had me cover by his grace he Established it before the founddation of the world, my emenies try to put all kind of interruptian like try ing to trap me But God show up for me every time, Psalm 91 verse 1 Those who live in the shelter of the Most high will find rest in the shadow of the Almighty, verse 2 This I declare about the Lord; He alone is my refuge, my place of safety; he is my

God and I trust him. For he will rescue you from every trap and protect you from deadly disease. When I was going up. This Lady my mom friend She was so funny she and her huband name was miss Bobbie Ann and mistard jakson they both was Laughable so funny in a nice kind of way miss bobie ann would shew her gum all day every day until the pont my brother JR was nine at the time ask her do you sleep with your gum. One time my Mother and miss Bobbieann went rideing on a ornery day and my mom seen too big garbarg cans in the middle of the street and my mom drive around them and miss bobbie ann said Darnele why you going around for my mom said Bobbie Ann did you see that too big garbarg cans in the street No I did even see those garbarg cans I would had too cans, rideing under my car and my mom laugh so hard and tole are family about, and the other time she fell in the hall closet over my family house wen my dad was there at the time when the jakson was over there for a visit that day see we had a walk in closet Bobbieann were talking and for she no It she fell right in the closet I thought was funny to my self MY dad was try ing not to laught so was daddy friend Bill came to visit too. Misart jakson pick her up ASK Her if she ok and all of us were consurn about her wellbeing but deep down in side we was had lots laughder to miss Bobbie ann was not hurt at all Thank God for that, that's was 1984 back in the days was fun times when my cosen toni was rideing with us and we went over the miss Bobbieann house my mom tole her don't stear at her she real funny she very laughable she will make you crack up Miss Bobbie Ann chewing her gum and talking very funny Toni was looking real close she was almost in her lap looking at her face with lagher. My mom said I tole you she is very funny to be around, This is a very funny story Once upon time miss bobbie ann was seting home watching television at night while her hursband was at work she hurt someone at her door she thought its was her son James she said james is that you she open the door all of a sudden she finely knew that was not her son James she look down the man did not have no pants on or shirt ether he just had a jacket on in flash her and Bobbie ann slam the door and lock it and shout out loud and and she made called to mistard Jakson her husband she said Jakson A naket man was at the door he said don't call me Bobbieann called the police, she love my

Renee Franklin

mother cooking she was pitcing off the lemon cake my mom made for
Bobbie Ann when we was over her house mistard Jackson was on the
telephones he tole her write down the telephone number and Bobbie
Ann was not even listening he look up and said you would not even
listing what I was saying I tole you get peace paper and write down a
phone number you busy piching off that cake Darnele made you those
was the good old days as I sit back and look at my cat gemi he remind
me of old cat gemi the frist he was a very smart cat too smart for his
good he would get In lots of truoble one time we brought him so cat
food he did like it he would cover it up with his other food pan lets us
no he would eat it some time my brother would go by him some cat
food because the cat would starve his self he would eat a hole day
unless you by the cat food he like sometimes the cat would bring a
chipmont from outside and run threw the house with the chip month
in his mouth we had to close all the doors in the house so he would
not get in are rooms MY Granmom was there to visit and she was
there when the cat had chase the chip month all over the house
Granmom got scard and jump on the top of the chair and finey my
brother darnell hit the chip moth with the broon and everything was
over Page 120 the cat stop chacing the chip moth and the chip month
was no more, and others times are cat gemi would boss my daddy my
mother would telll gemi way until granddaddy come home she says to
the cat the cat would get in front of the door and wait for my dad
come home and when he came home my dad would sit down and read
the news paper and he would say gemi the cat gemi would you doing
gemmie the cat would look at the door and start shouting out loud let
him no he won't go out side some time my daddy would not listen and
go back to the news paper and the cat would jump up and grabb the
news paper out my father hand and throw the news paper on the flood
and pull his paw over it and look at him and he let him no he meen
bussnes. One thanksgiving the cat got In the turkey he loves turkey see
the cat would get a table scaps of turkey from all of us he from me jr
darnell mom and dad the cat walk in the room and flap his self down
in the bed he slept for the whole day until turkey time again. one time
he wait until all of us went to sleep and the cat gemi has Is way on the
top of the stove of and he got in the pot and took the cover off the pot

124

and took that whole turkey out and got on the floor and had a feast on the turkey the next moring mom got up and saw the cat on the floor with are turkey she was not pleace with that cat my mom whip that cat and put him out side for hole day. That's the thanksgiving we never forgot, PAGE 121 I Remamber one time this man my father try to sposer A man from AA his name is Gene he was drugs bad and his mom put him out her house he had no place to stay and my dad wanted Gene stay at my house on the sofa that night my mom did not won't mister Gene in are house my mom had put her too sense and and are cat spoke something too in cat talk shouting to my dad too we were surprise the cat spoke his words My mom said even gemi the cat did not want him ther e ether So my mom put him out and mistard Gene had to sleep in the car I what not blame my mom mistard Gene were on drugs, my dad was only try to help but I say my mom did the right thang,. And I am convinced that nothing can ever separate us from God's love. Neither death nor life, neither angels nor demons, nether our fears for today nor our worries about tomorrow not even the powers off hell can separate us from God's love Romans 8 verse 8 I had a good day I was going threw storms but God is still in control I still press him my week was ok by the grace of God he allsume to me always he keeps his promies all of the time I went to my daddy house my family and I my baby brother birtday was toaday he turn 3 years old he from by father second wife we had a good time we had cake and Ice cream my brother had gilfe we had a good whole time my family am I and a old friend from school we grown up with back In the days we all had a good time, The love of God is with you in grace and peace in a time of trouble and turmoil remember nothing can separate us from the love of God-this is peace in the midst of the storm, by Peggie Moore And yet the Lord is waiting to be merciful to you. He is ready to take pity on you because he always does what is right happy are those who but their trust in the Lord, and yet the Lord is waiting to be merciful to you. He Is ready to take pity on you because he always does what is right happy are those who put their trust in the Lord. Isaiah 30 verse 18 Before talking about the word we need to read the guidance of God word and every day life. He will be our guide even to the endPsalm 48 verse 14 Believe in God no matter how your breakthrew has not come yet but still have a positive attitude seen like you running all over the community try to find a job and the people slameing the doore on you for me myself and I been there and done that but still God is amble to help me it is very painful when people hurt you having you believe they will help you but they just playing you along like they for you but really deep down they don't care if you make it or not with Jesue on my side I will make It and I look toward to a brighter future I will take of you Jeremiah, Jeremiah 15 verse 11 And the Lord replied, I myself will go with you and give you success. Exodus 33 versae 14 God Reminds us I heard your call in the nick of time; the day you needed me I was ther to help 2 Corinthians 6 1-10 So roll up your sleeves, put your mind in gear be totally ready to receive the gift that's coming when Jesus arrives, 1Peter 1 verse 13-16 with God on your side thing will sudden change, when people treat you like garbarg God turn it out for his good tressure, Now I will make your name as famous as anyone who has ever lived on the earth, 2 Samuel 7 verse 9 the Lord helps the fallen. And lifts those bent beneath their loads. The eyes of all look to you In hope Psalms 145 verse 14 Philipians 4 verse 13 For I can do everything through Christ who give me strength, verse 14 even So you have done well to share with in my present difficuhy, Page 122 one day I enter a contest but its was all set up these people were not right at all they protent they were for me but they were all agaist me they try to shame me so I could trop out of the contest but God is in control he is able to work it out and he did show up and everthing work out according to his plan. God reminds us I heard your call in the nick of time the day you need me I was there to help, 2 Corinthians 6 verse 1-10 But it Is good for me to draw near to God I have put my trust in the Lord God, that I may declare all thy works. Psalm 73 verse 28 well I past with flying colors my enemies was the one were put to shame and the people like my act That's was But God help me and I stole the show By God GRAZE made It I say, my foot slips your mercy, O lord, will hold me up. Psalm 94 verse 18 I see that the Lord is always with me, I will not be shaken, for he is right beside me, no wonder my heart is glad, and my tongue shouts his praises my body rests in hope Act 2-25-26 No, I will not abandon you or leave you as orphans in the storm John 14 verse 18

Taste and see that the Lord is good oh the joys of those who take refuge in him, Fear the Lord you his godly people, for those who fear him will have all they need. Psalm 34 verse 8-9 And the Lord replied, I myself will go with you and give you success Exodus 33 verse 14 Don't let your heart be troubled trust in God, and and trust also in me. When you have a Relationship God with you never go wrong and regardless what going on in your circumstances God have you cover by his grace and hope in my future look great. I will take care of you Jeremiah-Jeremiah 15 verse 11 you never saw him yet you love him. You still don't see him, yet you trust him with laughter and singing, because you kept on believing. You'll get what you're looking forward to total salvation, 1John verse 8-9 Dear brothers and sisters, when troubles come your way, consider it an opportunity for great joy. James 1 verse 2 If you need wisdom, ask our generous God, and he will give it to you t rebuke you for asking James 1 verse 5 entertainment of this world is not important we must focus on Jesue not the evil thangs but the unturnal things we can't not see stop loving this evil world and all that it offers you, for when you love these things you show that you do not really love God. 1John 3 verse 15 verse 16 for all those worldly things, these evil desire-the craze for sex the ambition to buy everything that appeals to you, and the pride that comes from wealth and Importance these are not from God they are from this evil world Itself verse 17 and this world is fading away, and these evil forbidden things will go with it, but whoever keeps doing the will of God will live forever verse 18 Dear children, this world's last hour has come you have heard about the antichrist who Is coming the one who is against Christ and and already many such person have appeared, the makes us all the the more certain that the end of the world is near, verse 19 These against christ people used to be members of our churches, but they never really belonged with us or else they would have stayed, when they left us It proved that they were not of us at all verse 20 But you are not like that. For the holy spirit has come upon you, and you know the truth. Verse 21 so I am not writing to you as to those who need to know the truth. But I warn you as those who can discern the difference between true and false verse 22 and who is the greatest liar, the one who says that Jesus is not Christ, such a person is antichrist.

For he does not believe In God the the father and in his son, verse 23 Page 124 For a person who doesn't believe in Christ, God's son, can't have God, the father either. But he who has Christ God's son, has God the Father also vers 24 So keep on believing what you have been taught from the beginning, If you do you will always be in close fellowship with both God the father and his son. And he himself has promised us this exernal life, verse 26 These remarks of mine about the antichrist are pointed at those who would dearly love to blind fold you and lead you astray verse 27 But you have received the holy spirit and he lives within you In your hearts, so that you don't need anyone to teach you what Is right, for he teaches you all things and he Is the truth and no liar and so just as he has said, you must live in christ never to depart from him verse 28 and now my little children, stay in that all Is well. And will not have to be ashamed and shrink back from meeting him, verse29 Since we know that God Is always good and does only right we may rightly assume that all those who do right are his children. I will save you; you will not fall by the sword but will escape with your life. Because you trust in me declares the Lord, Jeremiah 39 verse 18 o great and powerful God, who name is the Lord almighty great are your purposes and mighty are your deeds. Your eyes are open to all the ways of men; your reward everyone according to his conduct and as his deeds deserve, Jeremiah 32 verse 18 God king of Israel, your Redeemer, God of the Angel armies, says I am last and everything in between Isaiah 44 verse 6-8 My child your sins are forgiven, Mark 2 verse 5 for many are called but few are chosen. Matthew 2 verse 14 Obey the Lord then It will go well with you. Jeremiah 38 verse 10 this is a new beginning for me for the day God is so good he took care of me I believe he grab of hole of me and huge me and let me no he love me he spoke the word from the bible, the good book said to me Charm is deceptive and beauty does not last but a woman who fears the Lord will be greaty praised, reward her for all she has done. Let her deeds publicly declare her praise, Proverbs 31 verse 30 My troubles turned out all for the best they forced me to learn from your textbook truth from your mouth means more to me, than striking it rich in a gold mine. Psalm 119 verse 72 TMB, verse 73-80 oh love me and right now-hole me tight just the way you promised.

Steady my steps with your word of promise, so nothing malign get the better of me. Rescue me from the grip of bad men and women so I can live life your way. Smile on me your servant. Teach me the right way to live I cry rivers of tears because nobody's living by your book; you are right, and you do, right God your decisions are right on target you rightly Instruct us in how to live even faithful to you. Psalms 119-129-136 TMB, A call to live holy. So think clearly and exercise self control look forward to the gracious salvation that will come to you when Jesue Christ, Is revealed to the word, 1 Peter 1 verse13 TMB, VERSE 14 So you must live as God's obedient children, don't slip back into your old ways of living to to satisfy your own desires, you didn't know any better then verse 15 But now you must be holy In everything you do. Just as God who chose you is holy, verse 16 for the scriptures say you must be holy because I am holy verse 17 and remember that the heavenly father to whom you pray has no favor ites he will judge or reward you according to what you do, so you must live in reverent fear of him during your time as foreigners In the land, verse 18 for you know that God paid a ransom to save you from the empty life you inherited from your ancestors. And the rash some he paid was mere gold or silver, it was the precious blood of Chrst the sinless spotless Lamb of God verse 20 God chose him as your ransom long before the world began but has now revealed him to you in these last days verse 21 Through Christ you have come to trust in God, and you have placed your faith and hope in God because he raised Christ from the dead and gave him great glory, verse 22 you were cleansed from your sins when you obeyed the truth, so now you you must show sincere love to each other as brothers and sisters, Love each other deeply with all your heart, verse 23 for you have been born again but not a life that will Quickly end your new life will last forever because It comes from the eternal living word word of God verse 24 as the scriptures say people are like grass, their beauty is life a flower in the field the grass withers and the flower fades, but the word of the Lord remain's and that word Is the good news that was preached to you Because you trusted me, I will give you your life as a reward I will resue you safe, I the lord have spoken. Jeremiah 40 verse 18 Belive ye I am able to this Matthew 9 verse 28 Obeying is better than sayoing I'm sorry, Page 125

1 Samuel 15 verse 22 But Samuel replied what I is more pleasing to the Lord, your burnt offering and sacrifices or your obedience to his voice Listen obedience is better than sacrifice and submission is better than offering the fat of rams. We have to continue to obey God word and his will I regret wood I did in my past I go to God and repent of my sens when do wrong, to my family and to others people I ask God to forgive me on my everyday life Because we not perfact but we s erve a perfect God. Rebellion is as sinful as witch craft, and stubbornness as bad as worhiping idols, so because you have rejected the command of the Lord he has rejected you asking, So do the right thing and give to the Lord in prayer and obey his will Seek the Lord in prayer and repent of your sens he will save us with his grace for the Lord God is a sun and shield the Lord will give grace and glory no good thing will he with hold from them that walk uprightly. Psalm 84 verse 11 But they that wait upon the Lord shall renew their strength they shall mout up with wings as eagles; they shall run and not be weary. And they shall walk and not faitnt Isaiah 40 verse 31 Exodus 33 verse 12 I know you well and you are special to me, Trust in the lord and do good; live in the land and be safe seek your happiness in the Lord. And he will give you your hearts desire Psalm 37 verse 3 seek the Kingdom of God above all else, and live righteously, and he will give you everything you need, Matthew 6 verse 33 How precious o God, is your constant love we find protection under the shadow of your wings we feast on the abundant food you provide you let us drink from the river of your goodness. Psalms 36 verse 7 think about the things of heaven, not the things of earth. Colossians 3 verse 2 for whoever finds life and receives favor from the Lord but those who miss me injure themselves, all who hatr me love death Proverbs 8 verse 35-36 Listen, then and learn what the parable of the sower means, Those who hear the message about the kingdom but do not understand it are like the seeds that fell along the path, the evil one come and snatches away what was sown in them the seeds that fell on pocky ground stand for those who receive the message gladly as soon as they hear it But it does not sink deep into them and they don't last long. So when trouble or persecution come because of the message they give up at once the seeds that fell among thorn bushes stand for those who hear the message, but the worries

about this life and the love for riches choke the message. And they don't bear fruit and the seeds sown in the good soil stand for those who hear the message and understand it; they bear fruit some as much as one hundred. Other sixty, and others thirty. Matthew 13 18-19-20-21-22-23-Remember this my dear friends, everyone must be quick to listen, but slow to speak and slow to become angery, James 1 verse 19 take the teachings that you heard me proclaim in the presence of many witnesses and entrust them to reliable people, who will be able to teach other also 2 Timothy verse 2 An athlete who runs in a race cannot win the prize unless he obeys the rules 1 Timothy verse 2 Page 126 Remember Jesus christ, who was raised from the death who was a descendant of David, as is taught in the good news I preach, Because I preach the Good news I suffer and I am even chained like a criminal, But the word of God is not in chains 2 Timothy verse 8-9 That is why we must hold on all the more firmly to the truths we have heard so that we will not be carried away. How great is the goodness you have store up for those who fear you. Lavish is on those who come to you for protection blessing them in the shelter of your presence, safe from those who conspire Against them you shelter them in your presence far from accusing tongues. Psalm 11 verse 19 21 praise the Lord, for he has shown me the wonders of his unfailing love, he kept me safe when my city was under attack. Veers 22 in panic I cried out. I am cute off from the Lord but you heard my cry mercy and answered my call for help verse 23 Love the Lord all you godly ones; for the Lord protects those who are loyal to him, but he harshly punishes the arrogant verse 24 so be strong and courageous. All who put your hope in the Lord. Oh, what joy for those whose disobedience is forgiven, whose sin is put out of sight; yes what joy for those whose record the Lord has cleared of guilt whose lives are lived in complete honesty; when I refused to confess my sin, my body wasted away. And I groaned all day long. Day and night your hand of dicipline was heavy on me. My streght evaporated live water in the summer heat, Finally, I confessed all my sins to you and stopped trying to hide my guilt. I said to myself, I will confess my rebellion to the Lord and you forgave me. All my guit is gone therefore lets all the godly pray to you while there is still time that they may not drown in the fllood waters of judgment, for you are my hiding place. And protect me from trouble, you surround me with songs of victory the Lord says, I will guide you along the best pathway for your life, I will advise you and watch over you do not be like a senseless horse or mule that needs a bit and bridle keep it under control, many sorrows come to the wicked. But unfailing love surrounds those who trust the Lord. So rejoice in the Lord and be glad, all you who obey him shout for joy, all you whose hearts are pure Psalm 32 verse 1-2-3-4-5-6-7-8-9-10 I trust in the Lord for protection. Psalms 11 verse 1 I yes I am the Lord. And there is no other savior frist I predicted your rescue. Then I saved you and proclaimed it to the world Isaiah 43 verse 11-12 verse 13 From eternity to eternity I am God. No one can snatch anyone out of my hand, no one can undo what I have done. Verse 19 For I am about to do something new, see I have already begun do not see it verse 21 so my chosen people can be refreshed I have made Israel for my self and they someday honor me before the world. My Jouney for today was perfect my God show up by his grace I am save today Regardless what my circumstances I will still praise God he help me and in the past and I no God will help me in my future as well the outcome will be good Because of his kindness you have been saved through trusting Christ and even trusting is not of yourselves it too is a gift from God Ephesians 2 verse 8 Let not your heart be trouble, you are trusting God, now trust in me, There are many homes up there where my Father lives, and I am going to prepare them for your coming. When every thing is ready, then I will come and get you; So that you can always be with me where I am. And you Know where I am going and how to get there, No we don't Thomas said. We haven't any idea where you are going. So how can we know the way Jesus told him, I am the way yes and the truth and the life, no one can get to the Father except by means of means. If you love me, obey me and I will ask the Father and he will give you another comforter and he will never leave you. John 14 verse 1-2-3-5-6 trew 15-16 But it is good for me to draw near to God; I have put my trust in the Lord God, that I may declare all thy works. Psalm 73 verse 28 Preserve me, O God; for in thee do I put my trust. Psalm 16 verse 1 Thou wilt shew me the path of life in thy presence is fulness of joy; at thy right hand there are pleasures for evermore, Psalms 15 verse 11

Page 127 And he gudratees right up to the end that you will be counted free from all sin and guilt on that day when he returns. 1Corinthians 1 verse 8-9 God will surely do this for you. For he always does just what he says, and he is the one who invited you into this for you. 1 Corinthians 1 verse 8 for he always does just what he says, and he is the one who invited you into this wonderful friend ship with his son, even christ our Lord. For God hatch not given us the spirit of fear but of power and of a sound mind. 1Timothy 1 verse 7 All my Life I use fear of what may happen back then I did not belive in my self but God had my back every step off the way in my history he never fell me yet I am going threw storm but God is ample to bring me out and help me up when I fall. my Lord always has put all the pieces of the puzzzle together in my everyday life he is endless with God I wiil achive my goals in my life. If you put your trust in the Lord will never be put to shame. If the wicked put you by Embarrassment from hold lots of people when you going threw difficulty God will put them in shame. Who is that in the outer court. The king inquired. As it happened. Haman had just arrived in the outer court of the palace to ask the king to impale Mordecal on the pole he had prepared, So the attendants replied to the king. Haman is out in the court. "Bring him in," the king ordered. So Haman came in the king ordered. So Haman came in and the king said, "What should I do to honor a man who truly pleases me. Haman thought to himself" Whom would the king wish to honor more than me. So he replied "if the king wishes to honor someone. He should bring out one of the king's own royal robes as well as a horse that the king himself has ridden-one with a royal emblem on its head. Let the robes and the horse be handed over to one of the king's most noble officials, And let him see that the man whom the king wishes to honor is dressed in the king's robes and led through the city square on the king's horse. Have the official shout as they go, This is what the king does for someone he wishes to honor. Excellent the king said to Haman. Quick take the robes and my horse. And do just as you have said for Mordecai the jew, who sits at the gate of the palace. Leave out nothing you have Suggested. So Haman took the robes and put them on Mordecai placed him on the kings' own horse. And led him through the city square. Shouting. This is what the king does for someone he wishes to honor Afterward Mordecai returned to the palace gate, but Haman hurried home dejected and completely humiliated ESTHER 6 7-8-9-10-11-12 Surely you know that the wicked will not possess God's kingdom do not fool yourselves; people who are immoral or who worship idols or are adulterers or homosexual perverts, or who steal or are greedy or are drunkards or are thieves none of these will possess God kingdom, Some of you were like that but you have been purified from sin you have been dedicated to God you have been put right with God by the Lord Jesue Christ and by the spirit of our God 1 Corinthians 6 verse 9-10-11 Avoidimmordity and other sin a man commits does not affect his body but the man who is guilty of sexual immorality sins against his own body 1 Corinthians verse 18 No man is to have sexual relations with another man; God hates that. No man or woman is to have sexual relations with an animal; that perversion makes you ritually unclean. Leviticus 18 verse 22 in the end you will groan in anguish when disease consumes your body. You will say, "How I hated discipline if only I had not ignored all the warnings Proverbs 4 verse 11 if you want to find the road to hell, look for her house. Proverbs 8 verse 27 I no these people I ministry too about homosexual some thank me for telling them and other respond was not nice about it I got yell at in this company I use to work for back in the day not to bring the word of God on my Job no more even when I not on the clock, now some of the people who did me wrong at the time got fired at the time one person got fired for stealing from the gas stion one was taking to ER and and also got fired as well and other person got real ill I did not no who that person was that's person got black as cole the aids consumes that person body took his tole, When the storms of life come. The wicked are whirled away. But the godly have a lasting fonundation Proverbs 10 verse 25 Page 128 Pride leads to disgrace. But with humility comes wisdom. Proverbs 10 verse 2 when I going threw struggles and depression I have a close walk with God each day of the time praying and daily devotion keeps me going I look back on my memories what he broth me threw in my past and say why do I worried or get sad God is able to work it out on my behave on every day life. I think positive even my plan don't work out at the time is always is a brighter tomorrow that's my testimony trust Jesue and watch what happen keep on believing what you hope for when you got God he will fight your battles he willl show up on time He mite not come when he want to but will always show up on time. Jesus wraps this all up it's your faith. Not your gold, that God will have on display as evidence of his victory. 1 Peter 1 verse 7 you never saw him yet you love him. You still don't see him yet you trust him, yet you trust him with laughter and singing. Because you kept on believing, you'll get what you're looking forward to total salvation, So roll your sleeves, put your mind in gear be totally ready to receive the gift that's coming when Jesus arives. Don't lazily slip back into those old grooues of evil doing just what you feel like doing, you didn't know any better then you do now as obedient children, let your selves be pulled into away of life shaped by God'd life I Peter verse 8-9 and 13-16 a life energetic and blazing with holiness God said I am holy you be holy. Verse 17 you call out to God for helps-he's a good father that way. But don't forget he's also a responsible father and won't let you get by with sloppy living. Verse 18-21 your life is a journey you must travel with a deep consciousness of God. It cost God plenty to get you out of that dead end empty-headed life you grew up in. whoever rejects this teaching is rejecting a human being, but God who gives you his his holy spirit 1Thessalonians 4 verse 8 God wants you be holy and completely free from sexual immorality. Each of you should know how to live with your wife in holy and honorable pay, each of you should know how to live with your wife in holy and honorable pay not with a Lustful desire, like the heather who do not know God. In this matter then none of you should do wrong to other Christians or take advantage of them. We have told you this before, and we strongly warned you that the Lord will punish those who do that God did not call us to live in immorality but in holiness so then 1Thessalonign 4 verse 4-5-6-7 whoever rejects this teaching is rejecting a human being, but God who gives you his holy spirit. Make it your aim to live a quiet life. To mind your own bussiness. And to earn your own living just as we told you before in this way you will win the respect of those in this way you will win the respect of those who are not believers. And you will not have to depend on anyone for what you need, 1 Thessalonians 4 verse 8-11-12 Dear Jesue I am trying Everyday of my life try to walk like Christ like. Please help me to obey you in every step of the way, here my acoriding to my records I had a nerves break down I was kick use hurt abandon Laugh at spite in the face and all most fell in my life But God you were with me every step of the way but I am still alive by God grace I am still alive today Who has believed our message To whom has the Lord revealed his powerful arm. My servant grew up in the Lord's presence like tender green shoot, like a root in dry ground. There was nothing beautiful or majestic about his appearance. Nothing to attract us to him He was depised and rejected a man of sorrows acquainted with deepest grief. We turned our backs on him and looked the other way. He was our weaknesses he carried; it was our sorrows that weighed him down. And we thought his troubles were a punishment from God, a punishment for his own sins But he was pierced for our rebellion. Crushed for our sins. He was beaten so we could be whole. He was beaten so we could be whole. He was whipped so we could be healed. All of us, like sheep, have strayed away. We have left God's paths to follow our own. Yet the Lord laid on him the sins of us all. He was oppressed and treated harshly, yet he never said a word. He was led like a lamb to the slaughter. And as a sheep is silent before the shearers, he did not open his mouth. Unjustly condemned, he was led away. No one cared that he died without descendants that his life was cut short in midstream but he was struck down for the rebellion of my people. He had done no wrong and had never deceived anyone. But he was buried like a criminal he was put in a rich man's grave. But it was the Lord's good plan to crush him and cause him grief Yet when his life is made an offering for sin, he will have many descendants. He will enjoy a long life, and the Lord's good plan will prosper in his hands. When he sees all that is accomplished by his anguish, he will be satisfied. And because of his experience, my righteous servant will make it possible for many to be counted righteous. For he will bear all their sins. I will give him the honors of a victorious soldier. Because he exposed himself to death. He was counted among the rebels. He bore the sins of many and interceded for rebels, ISAIAH 53 VERSE 1-12 Page 129 that's the word of God, and he also says Come my Children and listen to me, and I will teach you to fear the Lord, does anyone want to live a life that is long and prosperous. Then keep your tongue from speaking evil and your lips from telling lies turn away from evil and do good search for peace and work to maintain it. The eyes of the Lord watch over those who his ears are open to cries for help but the Lord turns his face against those who do evil. He will erase their memory from the earth. The lord hears his people when they call him for help He rescues them from all their troubles the lord come to the resue each time. For the lord protects. The bones of the righteous. Not one of them is broken calamity will surely overtake the wicked and those who hate the righteous will be punised, but the Lord will redeem those who serve him, No one who who takes refuge in him will be condemned Psalm 34 11-27 For I am about to do something new, see, I have already begun do you not see it Isaiah 44 verse 19 Don't let your heart be troubled. Trust in God and trust also in me, there is more than enough room in my Father's home. If this were not so would I have told you that I am going to prepare a place for you. When everything is ready I will come and get you. So that you will always be with me where I am and you know the way to where I am going, No we don't know Lord, Thomas said we have no idea where you are going so how can we know the way Jesus told him I am the way the truth and the life, no one can come to the father except through me. John 14 verse 1-6 I have followed all his regulations I have never abandoned his decrees. I am blameless before God I have kept myself from sin the Lord reared me for doing right. He has seen my innocence, 2 Sanuel 22 verse 23 Remember this good deed also, o my God, have compassion on me according to your great and unfailing love Nehemiah 13 verse 22 This what the Lord says for I know the plans I have for you says the Lord, they are plans for good not for disaster to give you a future and hope, in those days when you pray I Will listen if you look for me wholeheartedly you will find me. I will be found by you says thew Lord Jeremiah 29 verse 11 Graduation you beem promoted Love Jesue the Lord and your saver. Listen says Jesue, I am coming soon I will bring my reward with me to give to each one according to what he has done I am the frist and the last the beginning and the end Revelation 22 verse 12 Happy are those who wash their robes clean and so eat the fruit from the tree of life and to go through the gates unto the city, verse 14 Once you received no mercy; now recived God's mercy. 1Peter 2 verse 10 Page 130 verse 11 Dear friends I warm you as temporary resdents and foreigners" to keep away from worldly desires that wage war against your very souls. Verse 12 Be careful to live properly among your unbelieving neighbors. Then even if they accuse you of doing wrong, they will give honor to God when he judges the world yet we who have this spiritual treasure are like common clay pots, in order to show that the supreme power belongs to God not to us 2 Corinthians 4 verse 7 I have the strength to face all conditions by the power that Christ gives me. Philippians 4 verse 13 in conclusion, my friends, fill your minds with those things that are good and that desrve praise things that are true, noble right pure lovely and honorable. Put unto practice what you learned and received from me both from my words and from my actions. And God who gives us peace will be with you. Philpians 4 verse 8 Don't worry about anything but in all your prayers asking him with a thankful heart. Verse 7 and God's peace, which is far beyond human understanding, will keep you hearts and minds safe in union with Christ Jesus, Philippians 4 verse 6 I am determined to to do the will of God No matter what come my way God have everything undercontrol he will bless me in his time no matter who reject you God says he will adcerpt. you I determined not to give up on God because he not give up on me, This is the Lord's doing it is marvelous in our eyes, Psalm 118 verse 23 I try to keep my mine focused on Christ Jesue committed to God is my life line my goats will take progress keeping and watching and waiting and praying and looking toward God is the answer. He will never abandon me or throw me away, obstacle may come But God will pursuid my goals on the right time and use people to bless me in the right place, you got to wait for your time, But when you pray go into your room close the door and pray to your Father who is unseen. Then your Father who sees what is done in secret will reward you, Matthes 5 verse 6 we have to believe in Christ Jesue who can do what he said he can do For a person who doesn't believe in Christ, God son can't have God the Father either. But he who has Christ God's son has God the Father also So keep on believing what you have been taught from the beginning, if you do you will always be in close fellowship with both God the Father and his son And he himself has promised us this external life, These remarks of mine about the antichrist are pointed at those who would dearly love to blind fold you and lead you astray. But you have received the holy spirit and he lives within you in your hearts, so that you don't need anyone to teach you what is right, for he teaches you all things and he is the truth, and no liar; and so just as he has said you must live in Christ never to depart from him, And now my little children, stay in happy fellowship with the Lord so that when he comes you will be sure that all is well and will not have not have to be ashamed and shrink back from meeting him Since we know that God is always good and does only right we may rightly assume that all those who do right are his children, Stop loving this evil world and all that it offers you, for when you love these things you show that you do not really love God for all these worldy things, these evil desires the craze for sex the ambition to buy everything that appeals to you and the pride that comes from wealth and importance-these are not from God they are from this evil world itself and this world is fading away and these evil forbidden things will go with it, but whoever keeps doing the will of God will live forever. Dear children, this world's last hour has come you have heard about the antichrist who is commming the one who is against Christ and already many such person have appeared, the makes us all the more certain that the end of the world is near. These against Christ people used to be members of our churches but they never really belonged with us or else they would have stayed. When they left us it proved that they were not of us at all But you are not like that for the holy spirit has come upon you and you know the truth So I am not writing to you as to those who need to know the truth but I warn you as those who can discern the difference between true and false and who is the greatest liar the one who says that Jesus is not Christ such a person is antichrist for he does not believe in God the Father and in his son. For a person who doesn't believe in Christ, God's son can't have God the father either but he who has Christ God's son has God the father also. Page 131 For this God is our God forever and ever he will be our guide even unto dearth. Psalm 48 verse 14 God is our refuge and strength a very present help in trouble. Psalm 46 verse 1 Give your burdens to the Lord. And he will take care of you he will not permit the godly to slip and fall, but you o God will send the wicked down to the pit destruction murderers and lious will die young But I am truting you to save me, Psalm 55 verse 23 O God have mercy on me my foes attack me all day long They are always twisting what I say they spend their days plotting to harm me. They come together to spy on me watching my every step eager to kill me, don't let them get away with their wickedness in your anger o god bring them down you keep thack of all my sorrows. You have collected all my tears in your bottle you have recorded each one in your book my enemies will retreat when I call to you for help this I know God is on my side, I praise God for what he has promised yes, I praise the Lord for what has promised. I trust in God so why should I be afraid what can mere mortals do to me Psalm 56 verse 1-2-3-4-5-6-8-9-10-11 We are ambassadors for christ since God is making his appeal through us 2 Corinthians 5 verse16-21 Since you have been raised to new life with christ set your sight on the realities of heaven Colossians 3 verse3 Jesue said I am the light of the world. Whoever follow me will never walk in darkness but will have the light of life. John 8 verse 8 Let all the world look to me for salvation for I am God there is no other I have sworn by my own name I have spoken the truth and I will never go back on my word; everyknee will bend to me and every tongue will confess allegiance to me the people will declare the Lord is the source of all my righteousness and strength and all who were angry with him will come to him and be ashamed in the Lord all the generations of Israel will be justified and in him they will boast. Isaiah 45 verse 22-23-24-25 The name of the Lord is a strong fortress the godly run to him and are safe. Proverbs 18 verse 10 Rejoice in our confident hope be patient in trouble and keep on praying. When God's people are in need be ready to help them always be eager to practice hospitality Romans 12 verse 15 Are any among you sick they should call for the elders of the church and have them pray over them anointing them with oil in the name of Lord James 14 in one of the verse Walk in the way of the good and keep to the paths of the just for the upright will abide in the land and the innocent will remain in it Matthew 7 verse 13-14 Wait on the Lord, be of good Courage and he shall strengthen thine heart: Wait I say, on the Lord. Psalm 27 verse 16 Know therefore that the lord thy

God he is God the faithful God which keepth covenant and mercy with them that Love him and keep his commandments to a thousand generations Deuteronomy 7 verse 9 Trust in the Lord with all thine heart and learn not unto thine own understanding in all thy ways acknoledge him and he shall direct thy paths. Proverbs 3 verse 5-6 It is of the Lord's mercies that we are not consumed, because his compassions fail not. They are new every morning great is thy faihfulness. Lamentations 3 verse 22-23 Thy righteousness is like the great mountains thy judgments are a great deep o Lord thou preservest man and beast. Psalm 36 verse 6 The sun shall be no more thy light by day neither for brightness shall the moon give light unto thee but the Lord shall be unto thee anto thee an everlasting Light and thy God thy glory, Isaiah 60 verse 9 My weekening was very successful I had good time I went on vacation tript we went on chunch Convension with my other chunch we went out my self and sister peggie Fransise Mother rose Mother betty Paster Lee his wife Sister lucy And there little granson Littie Jon we had very good time we left about 1015 in the Moring we on the road as we were past by we a lots mountains tops all around its something I never seen before. So the woman and I had connect we talk and Laught all threw the day about 5 we made back to the hotel everyone had a room the pastor and his wife and his son and the too mother of the church also had a room my self and I peggie Fransise we had a room also we went back to change for n at 7 the paster said be down stairs at 6 pm we all were down stairs n time. Sister lucy peach the word the service was alsume she pearch pray to young and old we had good time by God grace we had good time we were bless by the best that Jesue Christ the Lord. I will faithfully reward my people and make an eternal covenant with them, They will be famous among the nations, Everyone who sees them will know that they are a people whom I have blessed, Isaiah 61 verse 8-9 Page 132 we all us had good Fellowship all threw the day and after we eating from the restrant we all went back to the holtel and all us went to sleep I got up at 8am shower and dress and sister peggie and sister fransise went to eat breakfast downstaris and myself we had pancakes fruit and oatmeal and OJ AND Fransise had coffee and after breakfaust we all went back up to are room. They went back to sleep as for me I stay up and watch television and trying to my devoisiom at the same time and I forgot my jounal so I acts sister peggie was a gife shop down stairs she said it mite be so I went down to the hotel Lobbie to find out So I acts one of the worker at the hotel she said one the store is cross of street so went back to the room upstairs and got lost I did I no what floor what I was on But I for got the room number here I am knoking on the door saying sister peggie are in this room and paster Lee answer the door I said brother Lee I got lose he oh on and he tole his wife sister lucy called sister peggie come to the door Renee got lost then sister Yolanda one of the member chuch show were to go and sister peggie open the door and fransise were saying who is that she was sleeping and herd us she wonder was going on after I told then what happen we all had big laught about and I thought was kind of funny, it all work out according to his plan because I was not afraid Because I trust God. DO not be afraid Matthew 10 verse 28 Page 133 Psalm 16 in one of the chapter I will bless the Lord who guides me even at night my heart instruds me. Your callaufive for a blessing and your enemy no this and he watching you because he is in fear he no God has your back so he is trying to his best to break you. But God stept in every time, When you have God on your side you can't not lose. No weapon that is formed against thee shall prosper. Isaiah 54 verse 17 When going threw thr storms when people throw darts at us we cry out to the Lord My grace is sufficient for thee for my strength is made perfect in weakness 2 Corinthians 12 verse 9 No matter what come your way God have are life in his hands your under God's protected shill Happy are those who are persecuted because they do what God reqires the Kingdom of heaven belongs to thim Happy are you when people insult you and persecute you and tell all kinds of evil lies against you because you are m y f ollwers be happy and glad, for a great reward is kept for you in heaven This is how the prophets who lived before you were persecuted. Matthew 5 verse 10-11 I will speak out to encourage Jerusalem I will not be silent until she is saved. Isaiah 62 verse 1 I hold you with my right hand I the Lord your God don't be afraid for I am here to help you. I chosen you and will not throw you away Isaiah 41 verse 9 When everything is ready. I will come and get you. So that you will always be with me where I am. John 14 verse 3 Israel you belong to me alone you were my sacred possession I sent suffering and disaster on everyone who hurt you I the Lord have spoken Jeremiah 2 verse 3 Trust in the Lord and do good, then land and prospen Bridle your anger trash your wrath cool your pipes it only makes things worse before long the crooks will be bankrupt god investors will soon own the store before you know it the wicked will have had it you' all stare at his once famous place and nothing down to earth people will move in and take over; relishing a huge bonaza believe on the word of god the truth Psalm 37 verse 8-910-11 Those who have been ransomed by the Lord will return but now Listen to this you afflicted ones who sit in drunken stupor though not from drinking wine. This is what the sovreign Lord your god and defender says see I have take the terrible cup from your hands you will drink no more of my fury. Instead will have that cup to your tormentors' those who said we will trample you into the dust and walk on your backs Isaiah 51 verse 11-21-22-23 The Lord said they are my people they will not deceive me and so he saved them. From all their suffering; It was not angel. But the Lord. Himself saved them in his love and compassion he rescued them. He had always taken care of them in the past. But they rebelled against him and make his holy spirit sad. So the Lord became their enemy and fought against them. But then they remembered the past the days of moses. The servant of the Lord and they asked. Where now is the Lord who saved the leaders of his spirit to Moses, where is the Lord. Who by his power did great things through moses. Dividing the waters of the sea and leading his people through the deep water, to win everlasting fame for himself Led by the Lord, they were as sure footed as wild horses. And never stumbled. As cattle are led into a fertile valley, So the Lord gave his people rest, he led his proplr and brought honor to his name. Isaiah 63 verse 8-910-11 Page 135 God make it plain in his word. For I know the plans I have for you say the Lord they are plans for good not for disaster to give you a future and hope If you look for me wholeheartedly you will find me I will be found by you says the Lord. I will end your cativity and restore your forunes. When circumstances, come the word of God always has a amswer to are everyday life Scriptures is the main goal to look for without God word we wiil all be Lost in darkness When we go through trouble God is always in control when we go through trials. He will always place peace in are hearts When a man's ways please the Lord the Lord, he maketh even has his enemies to be at peace with him Proverbs 16 verse 7 and other Scriptures Bible Jeremiah 11 verse 13 if you obey the Lord you obey the lord your God and faithfully keep all his commands that I AM giving you today he will make you greater than any other nation on earth Obey the Lord your God and all these blessings will be yours But if you disobey the Lord your God and do not faithfully keep all his commands and laws that I am giving youy today, all these evil things will happen to you. Deuteronomy 28 verse 1-2-15 Unfaith people, don't you know that to be the world's friend means to be God's enemy" if you want to e the world's friend. You make yourself God's enemy. Don't think that there is, no truth in the scripture that says the spriit that God Placed in us is filled with fierce desires But the grace that God gives is even stronger as the scripture says, God resists the pround, but gives grace to humble James 4 verse 4-5-6 The Lord takes care of those who obey him Trust in the Lord and do Good. Live in the Land and be safe, PSALM 37 verse 2-18 What a joy it is to find just the right word for the right occasion Proverb 15 verse 23 and the land will be their forever Psalm 37 verse 19 Joyful are those who listen to me. Watching for me daily at my gates. Waiting for me outside my home For whoever finds me finds life and receives favor from the Lord. But those who miss me injure themselves, all who hate me love death, that's Proverbs 8 verse 34-35 I yes, I am the Lord and there is no other savior Frist I predicted your rescue then I saved you and proclaimed it to the world from eternity to eternity I am God. No one can snatch anyone out of my hand, no one can undo what I have done, Isaiah 43 verse 11 You will have courage because you will have hope. Job 11 verse 18 she won his favor Esther 2 verse 17 Before talking about the word we need read the guidance of God word and every day life. He will be our guide even to the end, Psalm 48-14 Page 136 For the Lord your God is amerciful God he will not abandon you or destroy you or forget the solema covenant he made with your ancestors. Deuteronomy 3 verse 31 how great is the goodness you have stored up for those who fear you. You lavish it on those who come to you for protection. Psalm 31 verse 19 blessing them before the watching world. You hide them in the shelter of your presence safe from those who conspire against them you shelter them in your presence far from accusing tongues praise the Lord. For he has shown me the wonders of his unfailing love. He kept me safe when my city was under attack. In panic I cried out, I am cut off from the Lord. But you heard my cry for mercy and answered my call for help, love the lord, all you godly ones foe the lord protects those who are loyal to him. That is why we must hold all the more firmly to the truth we have heand so that we will not br carried away Hebrews 2 verse 1 come back to the Lord your God. He is kind and full of mercy he is patient and keeps his promise he is always ready to forgive and not punish. Joel 2 verse 13 Now I am going to give you. Grain and wine and olive oill. And you will be satsfed Joel 2 verse 19 Who has done wonderful things for you. My people wil never be despised again. You will praise the Lord your God who has done wonderful thang for you. Jeoel 2 verse 26-27 Then Israel you will know that I am among you and that I the Lord am your God and there no other my people will never be dispised again, Y ou are coming to Chist who is the living corner stone of God's temple. He was rejected by people but he was chosen by God for great honor. I Peter 2 verse 4-5 And you are living stones that God is building into his spiritual temple what's more you are his holy priests through the medition of Jesue Christ you offer spirtual sarifiles that please God Page 137 Consider it pure joy. My brothers when ever you face trials of many kinds because you know that the testing of your faith develops perseverance James 1 verse 2-4 Perseverance must finishits work so that you may be maturs and complet not lacking anything. Be good to your servant that I may live and obey your word. Psalm 119 verse 17 But as for you, be strong and do not give up for your work will be rewarded 2 Chronicles in won the chapter These were all commended for their faith yet none of them received what had been promised. God had planned something better for us so that only together with us would they be made perfect Hebrews 11 verse 11 how I want to be there I LONG TO BE IN THE Lord's temple. With my whole being I sing for joy to the living God. How happy are those who live in your temple always singing praise to you. Psalm 84 verse 2-4 Psalm 84 verse 11 for thwe Lortd God is a shield the Lord will give grace and glory no good thing will he withhold from them that walk uprightly No good thing will he with hold from them that uprightly we mark by God Let us walk honestly as in rioting and drunkeness not in chambering and wantonness not in strife and envying Romans 13 verse 13 pure religion and undefiled before God and the Father is this to visit the Fatherless and Widows in their Affliction and to keep himself up spotted from the world. James 1 verse 27 Page 138 Philippians 4 verse 13 I can do all things through Christ who strengthens me. Psalm 56 verse 10 I praise God for what he has promised yes. I praise the Lord for what he has promised. Verse 11 I trust in God so why should what can mere mortals do to me. Isaiah 45 verse 24 the people will declare the Lord is the cource of all my righteousness and strength and all who were angry with will come to him and be ashamed. Verse 25 in the Lord all the generations of Israel will be justified and in him they will boast, the name of the Lord is a strong fortress the godly run to him and are safe, Provrbs 18 verse 10 Rejoice in our confident hope be patient in trouble and keep on praying. When God's people are in need be ready to help them always be eager to practice hospitality. Romans 12 verse 15 Isaiah 30 verse 15 This is what the sovereign lord, the holy one of Israel says only in returing to me and resting in me will you be saved in quietness and confidence is your strength but you would have none of it verse 18 So the Lord must wait for you to come to him so he can show you his love and compassions for the Lord is a faithful God. Blessed are those who wait for his help. Verse 19 o people of zion who live in Jerusalem, you will weep no more, he will be gracious if you ask for help. He will surely respond sound of your crieas, Because you trusted me. I will give you life as a rewars I will rescue you and keep you safe I the Lord have spoken. Jeremiah 40 verse 18 keep busy with the eternal one by obeying God by concerned above everything else with the Kingdom of God and with what he requires of you, and he will provide you with all these other things, Matthew 6 verse 33 Give to God, whineing or complaining Don't help seek the Lord and prayer and aks God for help. lots of people in the world go threw dispersion every day of the year more people end of killing they self or on drugs or drink to. about a billon people each day because they don't have Jesue in they live they have no hope in they life with out God there no voild in life to fill. Or some may have a nurvirse break down. They know God, but they do not give him the honor that belongs to him, nor do they thank him. Instead, their thoughts have become complet nonsense, and their empty minds are filled with darkness. They say they are wise, but they are fools; instead of worshiping the immortal God, they worship images made to look like mortals or birds or animals or reptiles. And God has given those people over to do the filthy things their hearts desire, and they do shameful things with each other. They exchange the truth about God for a lie; they worship and serve what God has created in stead of the Creator himself, who is to be praised forever Amen. Because they do this, God has given them over to shameful pasion. Even the women pervert the natural acts. In the same way the men give up natural sexual relations with women and burn with passion for each other Men do shameful things with each other, and as a result they bring upon themselves the punishment they deserve for their wrongdoing. Because those people refuse to keep in mind the true knowledge about God, he has given them over to corrupted minds, so that they do the things that they should not do. They are filled with all kinds of wickedness, evil, greed, and vice; they are full of jealousy, murder. Fighting, deceit, and malice. They g ossip and speak evil of one another. They are hateful to God, insolent, proud, and boastful. They think of more ways to do evil they disobey their parents, they have no conscience they do not keep their promises, and they show no kindness or pity for others, They know that God's law says that serve death. Yet not only do they continue to do these very things, but they even approve of others who do them. Romans 1 VERSE 21-22-23-24-25-26-27-28-29-30-31 Page 140 Then the Lord came down in a cloud and stood there with him. And he called out his own name. Yahweh the Lord the God of compassion and mercy I am slow to anger and filled with unfaling love fanithfulness. I lavish unfailing love and faithfulness. I lavish unfailing love to a thousand generations, and forgive evil and sin but I will not fail to punish children and grandchildren to the third and fourth genrration for the sin of their parents," Exodus 34 verse 7 Moses quickly bowed down to the ground and worshiped he said Lord if you really are pleased with me I ask you to go with us. These people are stubborn, but forgive our evil and our sin, and accept us as your own people. Exodus 34 verse 8 Don't be afraid he said take courage I am here, Mark 6 verse 50 if God be for us who can be against us, Romans 8 verse 31 here is God's answer to every guestion of fear. Certainly I will be with you no matter what guestion you may have if you know that God is with you. You need not fear Exodus 3 verse 11 I yes I am the Lord, and there is no other savior. Frist I predicted your rescue then I saved you and proclaimed it to the world. No foreign god has ever done this you are witness that I am the only God. Says the Lord. From eternity to eternity I am God, no one can snatch anyone out of my hand. No one can undo what I have done. Isaiah 43 verse 11-12-13 Fear not you will no longer live in shame Don't be afraid there is no more disgrace for you, Isaiah 54 verse 4 So he himself stepped in to save them with his strong arm, Isaiah 59 verse 16 He was Stepped in to save them with his strong arm and his justice sustained him. He put on rightewsness as his body armor and placed the helmet of salvation on his head he clothed himself with a robe of vengeance and wrapped himself in a cloak of divine passion. He will repay his enemies for their evil deeds Isaiah 59 verse 16-17-18 All nations will come to your light mighiy kings will come to see your radiance. The descendants of your tormenters will come and bow before you. Those who despised you will kiss your feet. They will call you the city of the Lord the zion of thr holy one of Israel, Though you were once despised and hated, with no traveling through you. I will make you beautiful forever, a joy to all generations, powerful kings and mighty nations will satisfy your every need, as though you were a child nursing at the breast of a queen. You will know at last that I the Lord, am your redeemer the mighty one of Israel. Iwill exchange your bronze for gold your iron for silver your wood for bronze and your stone for iron. I will make peace your leader and righteousness your ruler. Violence will disappear from your land. The desolion and destruction of war will end. Salvation will surround you like city walls and praise will be on the lips of all who enter there No longer will you need the sun to shine by day nor the moon to give its light by night for the Lord your God will be your everlasting light and your God will be your glory. Isaiah 60 verse 13-14-15-16-17-18-19 My Personal Story, way back in the days when I was going up I met this man we no each other since way back. I come to find out he was pipe and a drung added he try to have me to belive he was a good person but he was not nice at all. his communication was not right with me at all I try to tell Joe that's his name is not the way to live telling what God Says in the bible. Thou shalt not kill Deuteronomy 4 verse 17 But you belong to God my chidren, and have defeated the false prophets, because the spirit who is in you is more powerful than the spirit in those who belong Those false prophets speak about matters of the world, and the world listens to them because they belong to the world. But we belong to God. Whoever knows God listens to us whoever does not belong to God does not listen to us, this then is how we can tell the difference between the Spirit of truth and the spirit of error. 1 John 4 verse 4 I made bad choice being with him finalley I let him go I handle the problem the only way I no how to do We know that no children of God keep on sinning, for the Son of God keeps them safe, and the evil one cannot harm them, We know that we belong to God even thought the whole world. Is under the rule of the evil one We know that the Son of God has come and has given us understanding. So that we know the true God We live in union with his Son Jesue Christ This is the true God, and this is eternal life. My children keep yourselves safe from false god's, 1John 5 verse 20 Page 141 My handling the Problem. By praying and reading the word of God and obeying his will for the day and not look back what you did and the past is not necessary. but focus on your further is yet to come. We all make mistakes none of us not prefect But we serve a perfect God, by making mistakes make us a better person. We must not look back. No man, having put his hand to the plow. And looking back. Is fit for the kingdom of God. Luke 10 verse 62 Jesus answered, Verily verily I say unto thee Except a man be born of water and of the Spirit he cannot enter into the kingdom of God That which is born of the flesh is flesh and that which is born of the spirit is spirit John 2 verse 3 Like a example you got to chance your hole life stly by being Christ like we should not be frinds with the wicked Love must be completely sincers. Hate what is evil, on what is good. Love one another warmly as Christians, and be eager to show respect for one another Work hard and do not belazy. Serve the Lord with a heart full of devotion, Let your hope keep you joyful be patient in your troubles, and pray at all times, Share your belongings with your needy fellow Christians, and open your homes to strangers. Ask God to bless those who persecute you-yes, ask him to bless, not to curse. Be happy with those who are happy, weep with those who are happy, weep with those who weep. Have the same concern for everyone. Do not be proud, but accept humble duties, do not think of yourselves wise. If someone has done you wrong, do not repay him with a wrong. Try to do what everyone considers to be good. Do everything possible on your part to live in peace with everybody Never take revenge my friends, but instead let God's anger do It. For the scripture says, "I will take revenge, instead. As the scripture says if your enemies are hungry feed them if they are thirsty give them a drink for by doing this you will make them burn with shame Do not let evil defeat you instead conquer evil with good, Romans 12 verse 11-12-13-14-15-16-17-18-19-20-21 You will keep in perfect peace all whose thoughts are fixed on you, trust in the lord God is the eternal rock. Isaiah 26 verse 3 He humbles the proud and brings down the arrogant city he brings it down to the dust the poor and oppressed trample it under foot. And the needy walk all over it. Isiah 26 verse 5 verse 6-7 But for those who are righteous. The way is not steep and rough. You are a God who does what is right and you smooth out the patch ahead of them, verse 8 Lord we show our trust in you by obeying your laws our heart's desire is to glorify your name, all night long I search for you in the morning I earnestly seek for God for only when you come to judge the earnesty seek for God. For only when you come to judge the earth will people learn what is right. The wicked keep doing wrong. And take no notice of the Lord majesty verse 11 O Lord they pay no attention to your upraised fist. Show there your eager ness to defend your people then they will be ashamed. Let your fire consume your enemies, verse 12 Lord. You will grant us peace. All we have accomplished is really from you. Verse 13 O Lord our God others have rulled us, but you alone are the one we worship. Those we served before are dead and gone, their departed spirits will never return. Page 142 The Lord says listen now Israel my servant my chosen people the descendants of Jacob. I am the Lord who created you from the time you were born I Have helped you. Isaiah 44 verse 1 verse 2 Do not be afraid you are my servant my chosen people whom I love one by one people will say I am the Lord's they will come to join the people of Israel. That is where the Lord has promised his blessing life that never ends. Psalms 133 verse 4 come praise the Lord all his servants, all who serve in his temple at night. Raise your hands in prayer In the temple and prase the lord., may the lord who made heaven and earth, bless you from zion. Psalms 134 verse 1-2-3 They must thank the Lord for his constant love. For the wonderful things he did for them. Psalm 107 verse 31-33 They must proclaim his greatness in the assembly of the people and praise him before the council of the leaders, help us against the enemy human help worthless, with God on our side we will win he will defeat our enemies Psalms 106 verse 12-13 in the same way the spirt also comes to help us, weak as we are for we do not know how we ought to pray the spirt himself please with God for us in groans that words cannot express, Romans 3 verse 26 This story is expire by true story. So being courage be bless by the word of God I just one to let you know there is hope in the Lord. Do not give up. May God bless you in keep you in his hand. Thank you.

Printed in the United States
By Bookmasters